The Day I Learned to Appreciate My Ex-Wife

How I Let Go of the Past to Move Forward in Life!

David Perez

ISBN: 978-1-77277-064-3

Published by
10-10-10 Publishing
Markham, Ontario
CANADA

Printed in the United States of America.

Contents

I DEDICATE THIS BOOK TO MY FAMILY, AND ESPECIALLY MY EX-WIFE, ALTHOUGH WE SEEMED TO ALWAYS BATTLE EACH OTHER, IN THE END WE LEARNED TO HELP EACH OTHER TO MOVE FORWARD. THE TWO MOST IMPORTANT PEOPLE IN MY LIFE ARE MY SONS. BEING A ENTREPRENEUR I HAVE HAD MANY GREAT SUCCESSES AND MANY HUGE DEFEATS. IT'S ABOUT LEARNING WHO YOU ARE ON THE INSIDE AND BEING ABLE TO REINVENT YOURSELF

Testimonials

Riveting. David Perez captivated my attention the moment I saw the cover of his book. Immediately I had to pick it up, curiosity got the best of me. Looking inside and reading the first few pages I found myself drawn in. I could not put it down. Well Done!

Peter Seguinot, Doctor of Chiropractic

Empowering; the beginning grabbed me. I felt as if I was taking a journey with David Perez. WOW! The ending cliff hanger, exciting, I want more! When's the next book going to be released?

Wendy V. Marketing Director for Millionaire Mind

Amazing story of deep emotion. I felt as if I were there in the story, heartfelt, explosive, tear jerking! David Perez made me think about my own life and relationships. His writing ability is exquisite, I thought about how I treat other people.

Marnelyn (Jazmin) Pablo President/CEO of M&J Helping Hands INC.

Damn outstanding, it brought me to the edge of my seat. Could not put it down. Great read, what a story. A real life adventure!

Cindy Casselman Attorney at law, Corporate Counsel

ACKNOWLEDGEMENTS

I thank my ex-wife for helping me at one of the lowest points of my life. For opening her door to me and allowing me to stay with her and our children, when my world went dark. My family became the light that I needed, which inspired me to write this book, a lifelong goal that I finely achieved. After 15 years of being divorced, the 3 months I lived with her and my kids helped me expand my understanding and honor her point of view. I thank my oldest son D for his graces understanding, and his ability to tell me how it is! May this book inspire you to follow your dreams. To expand your knowledge and to give yourself the ability to forgive and appreciate other people for who they are. I would like to thank my youngest son C for lifting me up and listening. That helped me to battle the deep depression I was in.

I would like to thank Deepak Chopra and Oprah for their 21-day meditation webinar which I poured myself into, looking deep within myself to rebuild my life. I now enjoy a daily 20 minute personal meditation. I would like to thank the great author Michael Gerber, the author of "E-Myth" and the creator of the "Dream Room," for inspiration and taking the time for a photo with me. I would like to thank Raymond Aaron and Cara Witvoet for their help with the 10-10-10 program, inspiring me to push through the finish line and complete this book. I would like to thank Sumeet, my roommate, for opening up his door and renting a room to me. I would like to thank Valerie for helping me that October and giving me a place to live, which gave me the catalyst to finish writing this book. I would like to thank Meesha Sharma for helping me scribe my book. I would like to thank Professor Mary for constantly pushing me and inspiring me to write this book. Even though I sometimes didn't finish the homework she gave me, she was always a dear friend to me and gave a listening ear. I would like to thank Wendy V. for all her great energy and inspiration and becoming my friend. Most of all I would like to thank my Mom, Elayne Perez, for picking up the phone and simply listening to me, as I was in great turmoil and depressed in my life. Just knowing I could call you, gave me comfort in a place of darkness. Receiving love, light and hope! As a matter of fact I'm going to call her right now as I write this to thank her and tell her I love her, and let her know how much she helped me pick myself back up again. I would like to thank God for giving me the intuition to feel bad things before they happened, to guide me in a new direction in my life. I realize there is a greater path for me and I surrender to that power. Finally, I would like to thank you, the reader, for enjoying my personal story of healing, forgiveness and appreciation. Even though my book ends with a twist, the true battle between the black widow and the scorpion, I just want you to know that I found appreciation for my ex-wife and even to this day she is and always will be a friend of mine. Peace and Love to the world!

Foreword

I am extremely impressed by this powerful, adventurous, and deeply emotional book by David Perez. *The Day I Learned to Appreciate My Ex-Wife* is exceptionally well written and comes from the heart. David's amazing writing ability allows you to be transported into his story - you will feel as though you are right in the action! Your heart will pound with adrenaline and twist with emotion as you learn about his experiences. Your blood will pulse with excitement. I find myself craving to read more of David's memoir, and his ability to find good in all the negative that almost took his life! I could not put this book down until I finished it.

The Day I Learned to Appreciate My Ex-Wife will cause you to think back to key moments in your life and the way you reacted in times of need and desperation. This book will captivate you from the moment you open it - the first chapter will grab you with excitement, taking you on an adventure into the dark side of the medical marijuana business. You will then learn about an emotional transformation of David surrendering, letting go of anger and finding forgiveness towards his ex-wife. He learned to appreciate the only person who opened her door to him when all other doors were shut, being the light in a world of darkness! This book is fabulously filled with an exciting adventure, alluring emotions, and a cliff hanging ending leaving you wanting more, so take this journey into the life of David Perez, a memoir of 2015.

Raymond Aaron
New York Times Best-Selling Author

Summary

After three years of marriage my wife and I wound up divorcing. Things were happening too fast; we didn't learn to compromise, to support each other. We found ourselves in an epic battle (the black widow and the scorpion), a turbulent deconstructive relationship of selfish wants and personal needs on both our parts. I had hate and fury in my heart, and spent the next eighteen years of my life being enemies with the woman I once loved. Yet through all my turmoil, when everyone in my life turned their back on me, it was my ex-wife who opened her door and once again warmed my heart.....only to shut it again.

Chapter 1: The Beginning of the End

February 7th 2015 started out to be a sunny beautiful day in Mission Beach, California. I was renting a three bedroom, three bath beach house steps from the sand. At the time I was in the medical marijuana business, and basically worked from home. Little did I know my life would soon change. That day, like many others, my phone rang off the hook. Business was good and I was really living the life. I had my new Porsche in the garage, and my farm up in northern California was in full swing, producing income bi-monthly. I had a warehouse in San Diego producing income every three weeks. I was rising to the top, and fast. Money was no object, and in an instant I could make a phone call and have 20-30K in hand. I felt unstoppable. Angie, one of my trimmers, arrived at my house around 11:30 that day. Kane, my big Samoan buddy, had already been there since 9 am trimming. The day was like many others: drinking wine, trimming medical marijuana, and making sales. We ordered Mexican food that day, and I was waiting for my son Christopher to come over to stay the night. After 5 pm Kane went home, and Angie and I continued to drink another bottle of wine. Around 7 pm a friend of mine called me up looking for 4 lbs of mid-shelf outdoor medical marijuana. I told him I had it in stock, and we could meet up around 9 pm by the Catamaran Resort and Spa. My son finally made it over around 7:30 pm, so

I started cooking dinner and getting ready for my 9 pm meeting. About this time, I noticed cops all over Mission Beach and helicopters with spot lights. But living in Mission Beach you get used to seeing police all around, so I paid it no mind. I finished cooking the halibut with curry rice and stir fry broccoli, mmm. 8:45pm I told Angie I would be right back and asked her to stay at the house because my son was home. As I left I locked the front door, and began walking north down the front beachside alley to the Catamaran Resort and Spa. My friend and I had our usual meeting place on Pacific Beach Drive. Everything seemed to be normal, except the helicopters kept flying around and spot-lighting the area. As I crossed Mission Boulevard, I started walking east on Pacific Beach drive when I noticed a slender Mexican guy crossing the street in front of me. He came up behind me, and we both continued walking east. I rang my buddy on my cell phone to see where he was parked, and he stated "I am just a few blocks up." I looked back at the slender Mexican guy and noticed he had drifted back a bit, but it didn't raise any red flags, so I just gave it a "hmm.." Approaching my friend's car, I opened the passenger door and entered his vehicle. I had known this guy for over a year. We had done numerous business deals together, and I had a trust for him. We started talking, and I gave him a pound of medical marijuana to look at. Then he turned and looked at me and said, "Hey brother, I'll be right back. My friends are parked right around the corner, and I have to have them look at this, to see if they want it." At that moment, I knew something was wrong. Looking at my friend I asked, "Really? You've never had to do this before." I glanced out of the passenger's window, and to my disbelief I saw that same slender Mexican cat was approaching my side of the car door. He was just a step away; it all happened so fast. That's when my passenger side door opened up...it was the slender Mexican guy...with a Taser.. which he applied to my neck. Wow...the electricity shocked through my body. He hit me again with the Taser in my chest. I fell back into my seat, losing control of my body and melted, limping toward my so-called friend. As I gained back control of my muscle I said, "Bro, this is f'd up." Regaining my body, I realized the Mexican cat was still trying to Tase me, so my first reaction was to fight back. I grabbed his hand with the Taser, and I used my bag to wrap around it. Intensely I fought my way out of the passenger side of the car. The Mexican cat and I began to fight when his hand with the Taser freed up. Then he Tased me a third time. My knees buckled, my head became heavy, my shoulder went limp and I fell face first to the ground. I felt like I was in a nightmare and I couldn't run or react. Like a bad dream when you're laying there and your body is frozen. He must have hit me two or three more times with the Taser as I lay motionless on the ground. Stunned in great pain, regaining my body, regaining my mind, I could see this Mexican cat trying to steal my bag of medical marijuana. Luckily, I had it in my hand and fell on it while being Tased. I could see him tugging at the bag partially underneath me while trying to unzip it. My adrenaline was up, and I quickly realized I needed to get away, as I lay motionless on my face. The Mexican cat came at me once more. I then sprang to my feet, and hit him twice in the face and once in the body. I used my bag as a shield from the Taser. As I jumped up I saw some bystanders jogging, so I pushed off the Mexican cat, and ran stumbling towards them. The fierceness of my actions saved my life. I was tased at least seven times, and I managed to escape with my life and my belongings. I yelled, "Call the police, call the police!" but the bystanders just froze and said they didn't see what happened. I looked back and the Mexican guy had run away, and my so-called friend had sped off in his car. There was a pound of medical marijuana dumped outside the driver's side of the car that my friend had thrown out. The bystanders asked if I was ok, but I was still in a foggy daze from being tased over 7 times. I could barely walk and I quickly realized my life had been in great danger. I stumbled to pick up the medical marijuana that remained on the ground. Bruised, dazed and confused, I found my way home. I got back to my house, and Angie said frantically, "Oh my God David, what happened to you?!" I explained that I had been robbed and tased over 7 times, and asked her to lock up all the doors and secure the house. My son Christopher came out of his room and saw that my knee was bloody and the side of my face was bruised and bloody from falling on it, hitting the ground face first. I explained what happened, and I told them both to be careful. At first I blamed my friend; I thought for sure he was part of it. To this day, I still can't be sure. He did nothing to help me, and drove away with no regard for my wellbeing This was a set up; it had to be. Angie started to clean me up, and made light of the dangerous situation, which helped me calm down. I realized it was a good thing I was a tough dude, to survive a situation as rough as that. Angie cleaned off the blood, iced up some wounds, and poured more wine. Then three of my Chaldean friends wanted to stop by my house because they were in town shopping to buy a few pounds of medical marijuana. I explained to them to come over a different evening because I had just been attacked, robbed, and tased several times. It would be dangerous for them to stop by. But they insisted, and eventually I said "OK." A half hour later they stopped by my house with a nice bottle of Ménage a Trois red wine. I was cleaned up, but you could still see my battle scars. The right side of my face was swollen, I had a fat upper lip and a few scratches that were still bleeding. We talked, opened the wine, and began to relax. About an hour later, after I described the attack to them, they purchased their medical marijuana, and left through the front door. Everything was calming down when my phone rang. It was one of my Chaldean buddies yelling on the phone saying, "Hey bro, you set us up. We just got robbed outside of your house. As we walked toward our car there were 3 to 4 bald headed tattooed guys with knifes and baseball bats waiting for us. We had nothing to defend ourselves with, and they knew we had a bag of medical marijuana." I explained to them "It wasn't me and I had nothing to do with it." That's when we both realized someone must be watching my house. My Chaldean buddies said "We believe you, but be careful; someone is staking out your house." Angie's ride finally showed up to pick her up. It was now around 11pm so I escorted her to her car with baseball bat in hand. I knew now that another attack was possible, and my son Christopher was home with me. For our safety, I pushed the couch against the front door, and made sure all windows were locked. I moved Christopher and myself upstairs to the two rooms on the second floor, giving Christopher one of my long fishing filet knives and the baseball bat for his protection. I put him in the safest room in the house. I told him to "Use it if you have to, in case somebody comes in." I booby trapped the doors and stairs, and Christopher and I buckled down for the night. I slept in the master bedroom facing the front of the house. As morning came, the fog of the nightmare that occurred the night before had disappeared. We were both fine. My body was in great pain, and I had torn my right knee ligament by collapsing on it. I felt like a truck had run me over, and I had a hard time getting out of bed. Christopher and I got into the Porsche and I drove him to school. I explained the danger of what had happened, and the danger of the business I was in. I requested that he stay with his mom for a while. After dropping Christopher off at school, I went home and crawled back into bed. My body was now feeling the full effects of being tased. Every muscle was throbbing with pain. I was in great agony and really couldn't believe this had just happened to me. My mind was spinning; who could this be? Was it an attack on purpose or random? Who could have sent these guys? I knew this was a dark and shady business but this attack had caught me off guard. Tuesday morning, I called up Kane to come over early for protection. Kane was a 6′2″ 350 pound Samoan. He was my body guard, friend, and trimmer. We had known each other for over five years, and had gotten to respect each other. Kane showed up around 10 am, and couldn't believe what had happened to me. Angie came over at 11:30 am, and the day got back to normal. I mostly lay in bed that day, to heal my body and my mind. Angie joined me upstairs with her baby, and we laughed and made light of what had occurred the day before. Angie said "You got really lucky" and I acted like it was no big deal and I was tough enough to handle it. But deep down inside me, I was scared! Not knowing all the details, not knowing who these guys were, or who sent them, really put butterflies in my stomach. Kane stayed until about 8 pm on Tuesday, Angie stayed till 11 pm; Tuesday was all good even though I realized my house was hot and now I really had to watch my ass! Waking up on Wednesday morning I had a sudden flashback of a nightmarish dream I had 3 months earlier in December. In my nightmare I was laying in bed in the upstairs master bedroom when I heard the downstairs front door burst open. There was a loud wood splitting commotion. The master bedroom windows exploded, shattering glass into the bedroom. I vividly saw armed Mexican robbers coming through my front door and the master bedroom windows! Frantically in a pool of sweat I sprang up from my sleep to see if I was really in a dream. Getting out of bed I checked each window; they were all secure and not a scratch was on them. I headed downstairs to really make sure this was a dream. A sigh of relief exhaled out of my mouth as I saw that my front door was intact. At that moment I heard the house breathing; the walls seemed to expand out on the inhale of breath and cave in on the exhale. I was able to walk around a little, not sure if this was really happening, so I started to head back upstairs. I heard the house say in a deep yet silent voice "GET OUT, GET OUT." Chills ran down my spine as I walked back up the stairs to the master bedroom. Wow, what the hell was going on? Did I really just dream all this? Crawling into my bed I pulled the covers over my head trying to comfort myself. I could just toss and turn, toss and turn, there would be no more sleep that night. This flashback to my dream was a premonition of what was about to occur on this Wednesday. Kane came by earlier that Wednesday morning at 8 am to help trim and protect the house. Angie showed up at 11 am, and shortly after 11 I received an unusual text on my phone. It read, "A friend of mine referred me to you, and I need my dead-ends done." Before I got into the medical marijuana business, I ran hair salons for twenty years. Everyone knew me as the hairdresser. I wondered in my mind, "Who says that about split ends?"

Chapter 2: Grateful to be Alive

I had a bad feeling about this text, I had a bad feeling about the flash back of the premonition I had in December as I woke up this Wednesday morning. I then realized that in January on two occasions I had heard the house breathe and say in a silent voice "GET OUT, GET OUT." It made me realize something was wrong with this text and this Wednesday. The hairs on the back of my neck where standing straight up. Then I realized that this text was from someone who knew me. It was someone close enough to me, that I knew: they had my phone number. My phone started to ring off the hook shortly after 11:30 am that Wednesday, so I had John come by the house around 11:30. He was shocked, and kept saying, "Yeah brother, in this business you can't trust anyone. Everyone is out to steal and rob from you." We laughed, and John left with 7K of medical marijuana on the front, and to this day I still haven't seen John nor has he paid me back for the medical supplies. Chase stopped by around 12:00, and he took 10 pounds of medical marijuana (13K on the front) and left my house around 12:30 pm. Chase replied "Be careful brother, there's bad people out there." I agreed and we both laughed. Then Gabe called me around 1:00, so I met up with him by the 7-11 in Pacific Beach. Gabe and I talked, and he couldn't believe what had happened. I paid my debt to him, and headed home. That is when I got a very bad feeling that something was wrong. I couldn't pinpoint it, but my gut was telling me something bad was around. I pulled my Porsche in the garage; walking into the house I asked Kane and Angie if everything was OK. They both said "Yes." But I felt an eerie feeling in the air! That's when I went to the front door, closed the bottom half and locked the bottom door.

It was around 2 pm. I was just about to head upstairs when I heard my front gate open, and I said to myself, "That's odd, I'm not expecting anyone." I walked towards the front door to see who it was. Angie was on the couch with her baby to the right, and Kane was behind the door to the left by the bar counter. As I approached the door, I saw an evil looking Mexican guy all tattooed up, on both arms, reaching to open my front door. Luckily it was locked on the bottom part, but the top part of the door was open. I asked him, "How can I help you?" It startled him seeing someone at the front door and he stepped back, and changed his face... that's when I saw the gun in his left hand. The evil Mexican guy then came forward again and tried to reach over the bottom door to open it from the inside. I said, "Hell no" and slammed the door, shutting it on his arm. Angie, realizing what happened, screamed to Kane, "Kane, the front door!" Kane instantly jumped up and helped me slam the door shut. Kane was holding the top door, I was holding the bottom and the top. My body was in so much pain from being tased and my knee had no strength. So I collapsed to one knee... that's when I peered through the window seeing the eyes of the attacker, a black metal gun in his left hand. The attacker started to kick the door in frustration. He was frantically trying to kick the door in. But with Kane and I behind the door it wasn't moving. Between the 2 of us there was 575 lbs of muscle holding that front door shut. As I peered through the wooden shutters, I could see him stomping his foot on the front deck in defeat. He turned, calmly walked out the front gate, and headed to Mission Boulevard, with his hooded partner also carrying a gun right behind him.

I was stunned, realizing my life had just been in danger. Kane looked at me and said, "Who are these people? Where the hell did they come from?" I said, "I don't know, but they have evil intentions." Angie, with a wide-eyed look in her eyes, said, "David, what you just did in the last thirty seconds, saved our lives. Things could have gone really bad, and we could have been killed."

Kane, the 6'2" 350 pound Samoan who was usually brown, was ghost white in disbelief. He wanted to go outside and attack back. I told him, "No Kane, they both have guns, and I need you here to protect Angie and me." I then asked Kane to stay with Angie downstairs as I went upstairs to start packing up all the medical marijuana. Bag after bag, containers full, I even found medical marijuana under the bed that I had forgotten about. Then I realized how complacent I had become. The medical marijuana in my house was worth more than they would get robbing a bank. I called up my buddy Craig, "Dude my house just got hit, and I need your help right away. Come pick up some of this weight." I had just finished packing up everything, and started to head downstairs. Angie asked what I was doing, and I just told her I had called some friends to come over and pick up the medical marijuana. Angie screamed, "David wait! Don't move anything. They are probably waiting outside for you to do just that. Then you will be an easy target for them, so they can run up with their guns and take everything and possibly kill you." Realizing she was right I said, "OK I need a few moments to think." At that moment, Angie saved my ass. I started to realize that my dream in December was truly a message from God! Now I believe the house was really telling me to get out. Within minutes two chola girls, deep from the hood, walked by my house. Angie screamed, "These girls are with the two armed robbers!" She screamed again, "They are casing the house!" I looked out the front windows and asked her why she felt that way, and she said, "They don't look like they belong here. I can just feel it, I know these types of girls." The 2 chola girls stopped in front of the house, looked side to side, and moved on to the beach, Then 5 minutes later they walked back in front of the house, stood there for a moment, then went to the beach boardwalk and sat on the wall...not facing the ocean, facing my house. They continuously texted, and I knew they were lookouts for the evil Mexican armed robbers. That's when I said, "Angie, call the cops. These armed robbers are coming back, and with reinforcements. This isn't random. This is a crew. And they have a job to do." I realized that calling the police was going to change my world forever. But I would rather be busted for medical marijuana, than killed for it. Then Kane reported that he spotted another Mexican guy with a red baseball cap in the back alley, walking by my garage. I told Angie to call the police and let them know what had just happened, and to tell them she was here with her baby and two armed men with guns tried to break down the front door. Angie dialed 911 and described the event in detail. I was amazed at her detail and confidence. I fed off her energy, and I started to gain confidence. The 911 operator told her to stay on the phone, and that she had police on the way. Kane stopped and looked at me and asked, "Boss I really don't want to be here when the cops show." I was surprised and I feared a little, but realizing the police were on the way, I let him out the front door. The two chola girls were sitting on the boardwalk facing my house texting on their phones as lookouts. I thought to myself as I let Kane out the front door that this was my nightmarish dream coming true in real life. That's when I realized I had made the right choice! These attackers were professionals, they had a crew, and did these robberies for a living, for the thrill. These were bad people, they had no morals!

I shut and locked the door, moved the rest of the medical marijuana into the garage, and waited for the police to arrive. Within seven minutes, multiple police cars pulled up on my house. I opened up the front door, and walked out to greet them. At that moment I realized my life really had been in great danger, and that the attempted robbery could have gone really bad; we could have all been killed. Usually in situations like that they don't leave evidence. The police started asking questions, and I immediately stated that the two chola girls were in direct connection with the two armed robbers. When the police went over to question the girls they started to delete their texts. This made the police suspicious. The police then asked for their IDs and escorted them to their car, finding two loaded guns on them. That's when the police called for backup, realizing these were real players. Other cops showed up and started asking questions. Angie gave a description of the armed robbers, and within minutes a helicopter was flying overhead.

Each time a different police officer would show up, they would question me and Angie to see if our story was true. Then the lead detective arrived, and as he approached my house, he had a weird look in his eye. He asked me why my name sounded so familiar. He then realized he was the same detective that was on a case of a burglary in my prior home in University City, four months earlier. Somebody had broken into my son's room, busted out the sliding glass door, and robbed my house of approximately $10,000 in medical marijuana and all my electronics, leaving a blood trail. One officer at the Mission Beach scene approached me and suggested for my safety I should move out of the house that night. I had already packed. I was just waiting for the right moment. I asked the police officers if I could start loading up my belongings in their presence for the safety of Angie, her baby, and me. They agreed.

So there I was, in my house, police officers surrounding my home for protection. Helicopters were flying overhead, and over one hundred pounds of medical marijuana were in duffel bags and plastic containers all over my space. Yet I was calm, as if this was an ordinary day in my life. I again called my friend Craig to come by, and help me remove some of this product from my house. He called his worker Juan, and they showed up a half hour later. Juan pulled up to the back alley, and I ran to open the garage door. We started loading up numerous bags of medical cannabis into Juan's SUV. As we were loading up the bags, it dawned on me why these guys were robbing my house. I had way more product than I realized. We loaded up Juan's SUV to capacity, and they drove off to Craig's house. Within ten minutes, my grower Michael showed up to pick up the rest of the product. We then loaded up Michael's truck to full capacity. I was really amazed that I had filled two trucks. As Michael was leaving, the police officers were still standing guard at my front door. They had stationed officers around my house for protection. It was a surreal moment coming to terms with the fact that I was unloading multiple pounds of medical marijuana right in front of the law. One officer asked if he could search the inside of my house. I replied, "No, there's no need. I stopped the armed robbers at the front door." I must have had a guardian angel looking out for me that day. Michael's truck was loaded up and I told him to watch his ass to make sure no one was following him. Michael sped off to take his load to the warehouse. Angie and I were the only ones left. The police were wrapping things up around 5:30-6 pm. After collecting evidence, they had found that the two chola girls were on parole for assault with a deadly weapon, armed robbery, attempted murder, and carjacking. One was arrested with a loaded gun in her car, and the car was towed away. These were bad people. This seemed like an episode in the TV show "Sons of Anarchy."

I started cooking dinner for Angie and me. I had a nice halibut, I made some wild rice, and steamed some asparagus with balsamic vinegar and kosher salt. As the police officers left, Angie and I finished up our dinner and locked up the front of the house. I gathered up the rest of my belongings, and I put as much as I could into my Porsche, along with Angie, her baby, and me. The whole time in the back of my mind was the thought that the person who sent these people knew me personally, and had given armed robbers, a whole crew of them, my cell phone number. That made me very uneasy…knowing it was an inside job. I always heard of things like this happening to people, I just didn't think it would happen to me. As I drove away from that house, I knew I wasn't coming back. I realized my life had changed forever. Every moment, every second, I was afraid for my life. I could have been killed, we all could have been killed, and now I was homeless. Yet I was calm and collected, as I had to be strong for Angie. As I drove Angie to her mother's house, Craig called me to let me know the product arrived safely at his house, and if I needed a place to crash, I was welcome to stay with him and his girlfriend. Craig's girlfriend owned a mansion on the Bluffs overlooking the Bay and Pacific Beach, which made a nice hideout spot. I accepted, as I arrived, they started pouring wine. That night we all sat around in disbelief, and drank four to five bottles of wine (maybe more). When I finally went to sleep around 1 am, Craig and his girlfriend stayed up. Morning came. I was so hung over. Exhausted mentally and physically, my head was pounding. I was depressed, but grateful to be alive. It was Thursday, and my body was still bruised from being tased the Monday before. My stomach was in a knot, and food didn't sound good. My mind was swirling, "Who could have done this?" And immediately, three people came to the top of my list. The police had nothing to go on, and even though the two chola girls were caught with loaded guns, they couldn't be tied to the case. I called Angie to see how she was doing; we were getting close. We had a great friendship that was growing into something more. She was still in shock, and thanked me for reacting the way I did. Again she stated, "Your reactions in those last thirty seconds saved our lives. I don't know how I would've helped you, because I would have had to protect my baby." I agreed and we were both thankful to be alive.

Chapter 3: Remembering Hawaii - The Worst Vacation of My Life

I then called my ex-wife, to let her know what had happened and to explain why she needed to keep the boys at her house for a while. I let her know this was not a joke, and these people were for real; it was someone who knew me, had my cell number. Someone I had considered a friend. That was the first time I had spoken to my ex-wife in three years. Of course she reacted frantically and dramatically, but on this occasion I understood. This was not a joke; these were bad people with bad intentions. I called each one of my sons to let them know my house wasn't safe anymore. I told them that this was someone who knew me, so watch out, keep safe, and don't come by the beach house anymore. My older son and I weren't really getting along at the time, due to a disastrous trip when I took the family to Hawaii 3 years ago, where his mother brainwashed him by saying, "See how your father treats me? You would think he would respect the mother of his children," whenever she didn't get her way. Little did she know (or maybe she knew exactly what she was doing), she was dropping mental bombs. Needless to say, he wasn't very cooperative. He just said, "Thanks dad for bringing this upon us." My younger son asked if I was OK. I said "Yes, just a little shook up. It's not every day you get armed robbers at your door, tased, and homeless in the same week." I guess I was in shock.

Our family vacation to Hawaii was the worst trip of my life. I tried to get my ex-wife to stop badmouthing me while we were on vacation. I told her she was planting bombs in our children's minds. After listening to her for seven days, on the last day I finally blew up. If she didn't get her way, the first thing she would say was, "You would think that your father would respect the mother of his children." My son Christopher was her pet for the first eleven years of his life, but this changed on the Hawaii trip. Dante, being 15, was young, sensitive, and easy to mold. My ex-wife's non-stop manipulation finally sank into him like sharp teeth that wouldn't let go of the bone. By the end of the vacation I hated my ex-wife; I saw my son slip right out of my hands into the manipulation of his mother. The oldest son by nature protects his mother. My youngest son Christopher felt left out. He approached me and said, "Yeah dad, I can now see how selfish Mom really is." Christopher went from being the pet to being left out. So he and I buddied up. This was the trip that was supposed to bring the family together, but in the end it tore us apart. My ex-wife's self-indulgence drove me nuts, and on the last day I finally lost it. She was trying to push my buttons the whole trip. My youngest son saw this, but my oldest son was blinded by all the new attention he was receiving from his mother. For the first time in 15 years, he was first in her eyes.

The last day of this trip I wanted to go snorkeling and then up Haleakala Volcano to watch the sunset from above the clouds. She argued with me and insisted we go to the movies and watch Adam Sandler's "That's My Boy." Who the hell goes to Hawaii to see the stupidest movie in the world at 4 pm on the last day in Maui? We started to argue and I got upset that she was so selfish on this whole trip. She had charged up a $3,000 room charge in one week. This infuriated me. The kids insisted we go to the movies because it would make things easier. My ex-wife was complaining up a storm; pretending she gets road sickness. She even started to gag as an act for attention. We stopped at Panda Express for an early dinner. My ex-wife wouldn't stop. She just kept on trying to provoke me. She kept repeating, "See how your father treats me? You would think he would respect the mother of his children."(What she did not understand was that respect is earned, not just given.) So finally we arrived at the movies. We were an hour and a half early, so we walked around the mall and waited. My ex-wife and Dante were sitting together, and my ex-wife started to make fun of people in the mall. They would laugh at people as they walked by. I asked my ex-wife to stop this; it wasn't nice and it wasn't a good quality for Dante to learn. She just snapped at me and said I had anger issues, that I was emotionally abusive, and that I was trying to be controlling. I was thinking to myself, "Bringing her on this vacation was the worst mistake of my life." All my ex-wife was concerned with was manipulating and pushing my buttons. I just walked away and could tell I had lost my oldest son to her on this vacation. I still had a chance with my youngest to make him aware of what his mother was doing. Thank god he saw what I saw. As the movie started she was acting so fake. I started to get more irritable. Towards the end of the movie I had to walk out. Listening to that cackling hen of a woman, my ex-wife who was sitting behind me just made it worse. At this point I couldn't stand her tone of voice, the look in her eyes, or the smell of her skin. She waddled around like a lame duck. I waited in the car for the family to arrive. Right when the movie ended she texted me. She was being so obnoxious: "Where the hell did you go?" I was so irritated. She was starving for attention, and it drove me nuts. As soon as she arrived at the car I tried to bite my tongue, but she just wouldn't stop nagging. Then I exploded. A week of bottled up frustration had to be let out. All at once I yelled at her, "Stop. Shut the "F*** Up." Then I started yelling, "I hate you; you are not my friend. I can't stand you and how you treat me." Again I yelled at her about how selfish she had been on this trip. Yes, I really lost it! I never should have exposed my kids to that. That ten-minute ride to the airport was the destruction of my relationship with my oldest son. We arrived at the airport and it was the first time in a week my ex-wife had shut her mouth. I explained that I would return the rental car if she could check us in. I was furious. Blowing red steam out of my horns, the look in my eyes would kill you. When I returned to the airport, after returning the rent a car there were two airport police officers waiting for me. They both approached me and said, "Hello Mr. Perez." I stopped and asked them how they knew who I was; I never showed them my ID. They asked for my ID and I gave it to them. They started to question me, and stated they would escort me to the ticket counter. At that moment I knew my ex-wife had reported something to the police. I got my ticket and as I walked through the terminal, I could feel all eyes were on me. As I approached the security line, three security officers said, "Hello Mr. Perez; please follow us to secondary inspection." I then spotted my ex-wife standing in line with our kids. As I walked into the secondary inspection, I saw two regular police officers standing there. They stripped me down, checked and triple checked my bags and me personally. Nothing was found. Now I knew she had given false information to the police. The TSA agent then handed my ticket over to the police. As they approached me they started asking me questions: why I was in Hawaii, who I was with, and if I had engaged in a fight. I then calmly explained that I was here with my ex-wife and my two sons, to show them where I lived when I was 18. This was one of the greatest adventures of my life, and I wanted to share that with my kids. After talking with the police they said, "Hey brother, you lived here twenty years ago." I said yes and they handed my ticket back, and they said have a nice flight. I walked past the ticket counter, sat down, and started reading a book on spirituality written by Deepak Chopra. The TSA agent addressed the police saying, "That's him!" I heard the police saying "He's calm and cool, and has done nothing wrong." Within minutes I saw my kids and my ex-wife enter the seating area of the airport. My kids walked away from me; I motioned Christopher to come over. Dante wouldn't even look at me. Christopher shrugged his shoulders and said he couldn't. I knew then this wasn't over. I saw my ex-wife at the ticket counter talking frantically while speaking to a female flight attendant. There could be nothing good from this. I continued reading my book, as I tried to calm my mind. The stress she created was unbelievable. The head of security approached me with five big Samoan police officers. He stated, "Mr. Perez, please come with us. Leave your belongings and step outside." I knew this was serious if they wanted me to leave my belongings behind. The door opened, and I followed them. The moment I stepped outside, the five 6'3" 350 lbs Samoan officers got in my face, rudely asking me if I thought I was a tough guy. If I liked to beat up on women. If it made me feel tough to threaten children. I was confused and had no idea what they were talking about. I just knew my ex-wife was behind this. I stood there with the five huge police officers in my face threatening me. They were stating, "Make a move." " Go ahead, do something." I responded, "Do I look stupid? There are five of you and one of me. And you guys are huge! We are in an international airport. What do you think one man has a chance of facing five big guys?" They responded, "Are you getting smart with us brother?" I said no. At that moment the head of TSA agent approached me and said my wife had claimed that I was threatening her and our children with bodily harm and verbal abuse. I was stunned, shocked, speechless, and my mind was spinning. I felt dizzy; I couldn't believe what I was hearing. Then he started to say, "I am putting you on the no fly list. These are serious accusations. You threatened your wife and children?" That's when my mind came back, and I clued in to what he was saying. I interrupted him and said, "What did you just say?" He repeated, "Your wife is saying you are threatening her and the children." I asked him if she was claiming to be my wife. The TSA agent responded, "Yes. She is saying she is Mrs. Perez, your wife." Then I said, "Then her whole story is a lie. She is my ex-wife. If she is telling you she is my wife that is false information. She is delusional." In amazement the five huge Samoan officers dropped their mouths; even the head TSA changed his face. I repeated, "She is my ex-wife. So she is lying." They softened up and stepped back about five feet with a dazed look in their eyes. They resembled deer in headlights. Even the TSA agent asked again, "Your ex-wife?" I repeated yes. The five police then said, "Brotha, you took your ex-wife on vacation?" I said, "Yes, this was a trip for my children to have their mom and dad together. But she is so needy, selfish and manipulative that she turned things around." Then I asked, "Who is being more sane? Me sitting here reading a book about spirituality, or my ex-wife making a giant scene at an international airport?" The head TSA replied, "Brotha, why didn't you say something?" I responded, "I tried but you guys were in my face. You had listened to her, and I had to just be." Then another officer said, "Brother, I know how you feel. I have one of those. I would have killed her if we went on vacation together. What were you thinking?" I guess I didn't really think it all the way through. Then another one said, "Yeah bro, I got one of those."

We all had a small moment of brotherhood. All five officers, the TSA agent, and I all had ex-wives. One officer even said, "I know how you feel, I have two ex-wives!" I said, "What, you didn't learn the first time?" He said, "Hey brother, you took yours on vacation."

We all laughed and calmed down for a moment. They knew I was telling the truth. Then a flight attendant came over and pointed to me and exclaimed, "That's him. That's him!" The head TSA agent told her the situation, and she stormed back to the counter. The TSA agent walked back over saying "We believe you, but we can't let you fly home on the same plane." I said, "Well I have clients booked for tomorrow, and I need to fly home. Maybe my ex-wife can stay because she made up the whole thing." The agent asked her, but of course she refused. He came back and said, "Look brother, we don't want any trouble. An easy solution for me would be for you to get you a hotel room and fly you out first thing in the A.M." I told him he was the boss, and if that's what he needed me to do, then it's done. He said, "Bro we're not even going to put you on the no-fly list. Matter of fact, we're not even going to report this. We all have ex-wives and we understand what you are going through. Just be here tomorrow at 12:30 pm to take the 1:30 pm flight home." I said OK and thanked him for understanding. He said no problem, but the police officers would have to escort me out of the airport. I was able to pick up my bags, and was then escorted off the airport property. They had a van waiting for me to take me to Hilton for the night. By now it was around 6 pm. So I had dinner and sat at the bar with a few Heinekens. I couldn't believe how bad this Hawaii trip had gone. I couldn't believe how much she refused to compromise. Out of seven days in Hawaii it took us until the last day to go on a family outing; a snorkel cruise. It was the best part of the trip, but right after the cruise she acted out yet again. I couldn't believe how selfish and inconsiderate she was being. I knew why I divorced this woman. I really did hate her. I could see how manipulative she was. How she wanted to be put on a pedestal. She expected and demanded, which made me feel like ignoring her.

After returning home from our Hawaii vacation I decided to close my salon for good. I didn't care anymore, and my ex-wife's manipulation had taken its toll. This was our divorce all over again. The trip to Hawaii wound up costing me nearly $20,000 for one week. When we got home my ex-wife hired an attorney claiming I had buried cash and was hiding money. She didn't believe I was going bankrupt, even though I had filed for bankruptcy. My ex-wife filed a lawsuit asking for more child support, and 100% custody of the children. She had called child protective services; she went as far as reporting me as if I did not pay her child support, with child support services. This was over the top for me. I was mentally done. I didn't care anymore. The only thing I knew was she was not getting more money. That is when I decided to walk away from my life. I was under great pressure, but she still didn't care about me, just the money.

Chapter 4: Surrendering and Appreciating

Day 2 at Craig's house, After the attack at my house, the wine was still flowing. We drank our hearts out. I couldn't believe how much wine Craig and his girlfriend consumed. It wasn't even dinner time and we already polished off four bottles of wine. It wasn't helping. It was bringing me down, and hard. I was depressed. I couldn't think clearly. Who hated on me so much to bring this upon me? It just made me confused and I wondered all day. The third day came, and again by 5 pm we were on our fifth bottle of wine. I was just thankful to be alive, to have a roof over my head, a place to stash my cannabis, and my duffel bag of cash. Saturday was a busy day. Craig had been drunk for three days, and was letting people in and out of his house. This made me feel very uncomfortable considering what had just happened to me. Around 8 pm we all decided to go out for dinner (and more wine). We went to Craig's favorite spot at the beach, there were six of us, and a few bottles of vino. We were all still discussing how lucky I had been, that I was still alive. I must have had a few guardian angels that day. Craig's phone rang and I overheard him telling people to drop off the medical marijuana at his house. I reached over and spoke with Craig, "Hey brother, I have a lot of medical marijuana and cash at your house, and it is making me feel uneasy how you're just letting people come through there." Craig replied, "No worries man, these are my friends, and I am responsible for everything in my house." I said, "Thank you, but that is all the cash I have to my name." More wine was ordered, we finished dinner, and we moved to the bar dance floor. By now we were all very well drunk. Then the shots of Don Julio came, and that was it. Oh, how I love tequila. The first shot warmed my heart and my stomach, so we ordered more. By the 6th shot, I was feeling no pain. By now Craig and his girlfriend had already gone home but Craig's friend stayed behind, and him and I continued to drink. We must've done 9 shots. I was drunk. We took a taxi home, and as I walked into Craig's house I saw it was full of drunk people. That is when my mind freaked out. I was intoxicated and realizing I had over 40K+ upstairs in a duffel bag, and about 100 pounds of medical marijuana in his garage. I then went upstairs to check on my money, and it was gone. I ran downstairs, "Where the "F" is my money?" All my belongings were moved out of my room, and Craig was trying to calm me down. But after the week I had, all the wine, and the shots of tequila, I lost it. After an hour of me yelling "Where the "F" is my money?!" we finally found the money that Craig's girlfriend's- friend had taken out of my room along with all my things, and had put in the garage without telling anyone so she could use that room that night. Then Craig said I had to leave, and I wasn't welcome in his house anymore. It was hard for me to calm down. So I left the medical marijuana, took the cash, and drove off in my Porsche. I realized I was too drunk to drive, and parked my Porsche a few streets down from Craig's house, and passed out. If you have ever tried to sleep in a Porsche, you know this is almost impossible. Yet somehow I managed. As the sun came up, I felt it beating on my face. My head was pulsating. My back was sore. My face was swollen. So I drove to the beach.

Hung over I laid out my yoga mat, and rested on the beach for two hours… still drunk, from the night before, with nowhere to go. Around 10:30 am, when the sun finally made it up, there were no more shadows on the beach for me to hide in the sun was starting to heat up the day. I don't know why I got into my Porsche, but I drove to my ex-wife's house. I arrived and opened up the unlocked front door. She stood in the living room, freaking out, "Get out, get out, you are putting us in danger!" I just said to her, "I need to crash and heal for a little bit." My body was still badly bruised from being tased, the three days of drunkenness, the thugs who were armed with guns trying to kick down my door, and everything was just getting worse. I walked by my ex-wife through the living room without listening to her, and crashed on my oldest son's bed. My ex kept coming into the room screaming, "Why are you here?" Truthfully, I had nowhere to go. In a instance my life had changed. I closed my eyes and just passed out.

Next thing I knew morning came. I must have slept more

than 24 hours. My body was in more pain than any other day. My mind was depressed. I tried to eat. I was still afraid. That day my ex-wife was screaming and yelling. I could barely move my body. My oldest son came into his room and said, "Dad. I need my room back." I explained, "Son, give me a break. A lot has happened in the last few days." After a couple of hours of listening to my son and my ex-wife complaining, I moved to the couch in the living room. Alia, my ex-wife's best friend, told her "Just leave him alone, he's drunk, he'll be ok." I put the TV on, got a pillow, lay down a blanket, and started to heal my body. I could still feel the tension in the house; everyone, especially me, was afraid of someone trying to attack me at this house. But I knew everyone who knew me also knew I couldn't stand my ex-wife, and that we had not been on speaking terms for years. Ever since our horrible family vacation to Hawaii. That made me realize her house was truly a safety zone for me. No one would ever expect me hiding out at my ex-wife's house. I just had to put up listening to her frantically screaming and yelling. She reminded me of the teacher from Charlie Brown, "Wah. Wah. Wah. Wah." After two or three days, I don't really remember, we all started to settle in, and things calmed down a little. But we were still fighting like cats and dogs. I realized she was just trying to protect our children. My life had gotten to be crazy, dangerous, and lonely. Then the fire alarm went off in the living room, and my ex-wife came screaming out of her room, "Turn it off, turn it off!" The tone of her voice triggered me to react. All

I could do was yell at her to stop screaming. My son yelled at me to calm down. At that moment I realized we were in a cycle. It was the pitch of her voice that irritated the hell out of me. We had fallen back into our old relationship pattern from when we were married. I was thinking at that time it was a mistake for me to be there, but I had no options. A lot of my friends had deserted me, and even my ex-girlfriend Jen told me to lose her number. I truly had nowhere else to turn. After the fire alarm issue, I started to really think about myself and what it was about my ex-wife that triggered me. I wondered how I could avoid this in the future, knowing I had no other options, and I had to make this work. As night came, my ex-wife was in her room, my sons were in their room, and I lay on the couch. My head was still pounding, and my body was in great pain. I could barely move my right knee. We all fell asleep. In the morning, it must have been the fourth or fifth day, my ex-wife woke up in a really bad mood. She started ranting and raving about how I needed to move out and find my own place. I could barely walk. Still in the medical marijuana business, I knew I could get right back on my feet again. I could tell the whole robbery business really made my ex-wife feel unsafe. By the fifth day she was almost attacking me. On that day, she had been upset for an easy three to four hours in the morning. Finally, when she walked into the living room she started yelling at me. I responded, "I forgive you for everything. From this day forward, I only have warmth in my heart for you." That stopped her dead in her tracks. She turned and looked at me, eyes wide open, and asked, "What did you just say?" I repeated, "I forgive you for everything. And from this day forward, I only have warmth in my heart for you. Thank you for helping me when I needed it the most." And that is the day I learned to appreciate my ex-wife.

That morning I realized I had to surrender my feelings. I had to surrender my thoughts, and my ego, in order for this to work. We had not spoken in three years, since I took her and the kids on that disastrous trip to Hawaii. It pulled our family apart. My oldest son had not spoken to me in three years, and my life was consumed with anger. That was the real beast in all of my misfortunes. Every time I let my anger out, it destroyed another good part of my life. It was my ego that allowed this beast to arrive. This day I learned a real appreciation for my ex-wife. The truth was, what she was doing was a huge favor. In the midst of my darkness, it was my ex-wife who opened her door, and brought some light into my life. Imagine that all you can see is darkness, sadness, loneliness, and depression. You almost lost your life. Your whole world has just changed overnight. And in your darkest point, a door opens, beaming light. My ex-wife told me, "It's me who should be forgiving you!" And I said, "Just accept the compliment. This is why we fight." She looked away and walked into her room. A few hours later she emerged, a whole new woman. It was tough at first to control my mouth and my anger; she knew how to push my buttons. Yet something inside of me said just be kind, smile and give her a compliment. Things like, "That's a nice color on you." "That shirt looks good on you." "Those flowers in your hair are nice." It was the simplest details that I had always overlooked that she cared about the most. It wasn't the home run, or the fancy night out that really made her happy. Make no mistake, she loved that just as well. But by surrendering my ego, I had different thoughts, a different approach, and a different outlook as a human being. This battle was internal. Only I could save myself. It was the simplest compliments that made her shine. I would give her a compliment and notice her being grateful. Her face would smile, her eyes would open wider. Her shoulders would engage back, raising her heart up. I could even see her light beaming a little brighter. This was fascinating to me. The more I complimented, the better we got along. Now remember, this was my arch enemy for eighteen years of my life. Yet in the worst moment of my life, somehow, we became friends again. I couldn't believe this was happening. How could I really let go of all the hatred and anger I had for her? I despised her. I was so angry about our divorce. I was angry about how she had me put in jail when we first got married, after she attacked me and told the police I hit her (which was a untrue statement, to the police). I was angry about how she tried to take away my children, going for 100% custody, and tried to control my time with them during or divorce. I was angry she had made false statements to the police. I was angry she had taken my house, and I had to live in a studio. I was angry she was asking for $8,000 a month to live on. There were many other issues that I realized I was still holding on to. It truly took losing everything for me to open my eyes and to see more clearly. To see what was important in life. And suddenly the most important thing was to make amends with my ex-wife. To bring peace to my immediate family; my children, myself, and her. To grow as a person. Forgiving my ex-wife was, in a way, forgiving myself. I didn't realize how much I was holding on to, and how it was destroying me as a person. It made me bitter and changed my energy, my aura. By learning to appreciate my ex-wife I began to see things differently; I became more grateful. I learned to appreciate myself! But I had to figure out what triggered me. That night I took her out to dinner and we talked. I opened up about writing this book, and how my original goal was to finish this book and give it to her when I moved out. Then I realized two brains are better than one. So that night I invited her to join me on the journey to accomplish this book. When I told her my idea she was amazed; she asked me why I would want to write it and what the title would be. I said it would be "The Day I Learned to Appreciate my ex-wife." She was in awe, she started to tear up and said, "That's amazing." She reached for her heart and told me how thoughtful I am. At that moment I realized that she was the better half. She added softness to my hardness, she added additional words to my shortness, she added beauty to a room with her big beautiful eyes. As we talked over dinner we both got emotional. I realized that I had made the right decision to have her help me write this book. She had a different view with different emotions. She had the sugar and I had the spice. Dinner got more interesting and our conversation started to grow. We both brought up new ideas and things that had occurred in our past relationship. How when I felt she was attacking me, she was merely trying to get my attention. One of my clients once told me, "What men consider nagging, women consider caring." And this was how my ex-wife saw things. She was only caring about me as she took me to court countless times for more money (being sarcastic). Forgiveness is the greatest thing besides love. To truly forgive someone, you have to really look inside yourself to see the reflection of what you don't like about that person. Usually it is a part of you that is the real reason why someone else irritates you. By forgiving someone you are letting go of the past; you are entering your present.

As children we receive presents and our energy changes with joy to see what is inside the beautifully wrapped box. The same can be said about forgiveness; it is a gift that you receive with big open eyes, so thankful. Holding onto issues only creates bad energy, and people around you can see the negative vibe. As men we tend to hold on to things and bury them, which turns them into triggers. Men are not good communicators, which is why we tend to stuff our feelings down deep. In our minds we think we show weakness when we communicate. But as we grow, we become comfortable showing our weaker side, making us better men. This is how I learned to surrender my emotions to my ex-wife. To allow her to be emotional, to express her feelings, to allow her to critique me, and add to me.

We ordered another glass of wine, and she became very thankful and motivated. Once again, we were connecting, and it was beautiful. It was amazing to have this woman, my worst enemy, become my best friend. To share warmth with the mother of my children was a truly magical moment. My ex-wife reached over to hold my hand, and I realized a lot of her fighting was her trying to reach into my feelings. As a man they were too deep down, it made it hard for her to reach in and connect to them. It created a block in our relationship. By learning to appreciate my ex-wife, I learned to open up my soul, to eliminate the blocks, to clear my energy, and to simply surrender to her needs and emotions.

If only all men could realize how important all this appreciation, forgiveness, warmth, and love is to a woman, and truly to a man and his family. Times have changed, and men are now playing in a different field. Women have become more equal in the eyes of society, and communication is a must for any relationship or friendship. I see now why we fought. It was my ego as a man that clouded up my mind, disabling me to achieve good communication, understanding, and compromise. In the end my ex-wife never found time to help out with this book. It is interesting to reflect how we thought as young adults versus how we think in our mid-forties, and what we have gathered. Time really heals. But my recommendation is to get to know your inner self, to feel your emotions, to hear your heart. Don't listen to your ego or anger. Enjoy your softer side, be human. Take a chance and just let go. By letting go you allow for the bad feelings and emotions to release, opening a path for new and better things to come into your life. Remove the blocks, open up your doors, and you will be amazed at how things will change in your relationships. Even after I learned to appreciate my ex-wife, I still had to learn about how to appreciate her for who she truly is. I had to accept her frantic mood swings due to her depression, I had to accept her high pitched tone of voice (which was a trigger for me), I had to accept her laziness, and her ability to sleep all day (which drove me nuts) realizing these where symptoms of her emotional state. When you start to see someone for who they really are, inside and out, you really start to see their true beauty. I personally feel most people only see externally; they lose sight of a person's inner beauty. Going through what I went through in 2015, I realized I had to see differently. I realized how my old self was no longer serving me. I had to open up my personal inner doors. Now I am focused on creating my new self, full of forgiveness, appreciation, happiness, and love. I am writing this book for my ex-wife, so she can now see my inner beauty, and how I have gained respect, admiration, and love for the mother of my children. Like I said, I too am still learning how to achieve this on a daily basis; and that is one day at a time. I still have moments when I feel she is attacking me. The other night as we were driving home from dinner, after taking her out for Italian food, she slipped into an old relationship pattern of refusing responsibility and placing blame on me.. As we drove home, she began pointing out my broken relationships with my father, brother, and sister. She told me it was all my fault due to my anger issues, and at the moment I could see my old self wanting to reach out, grab her by the neck and shake some sense into her. As I caught my old self, I inhaled a positive thought and exhaled my old self out. I started to realize that there was some truth in her words, and that was what made me angry and triggered me to react and visualize. It was the angry beast once again out of his cage; the same beast that ultimately turned my family, my oldest son and my ex-wife into people I had no relationship with. So, yes, there was some truth in her placing the blame on me. I accepted that fact, and the responsibility of yelling, being angry, and releasing the beast upon my family. I haven't actually spoken to them in many years. I have tried to reach out, but it has been a very one-sided approach. I realized that for them to not want to talk to me, I must have really hurt their feelings. And for that I am very sorry. What is truly amazing, is my ex-wife. For all the times she has seen the beast, and had to engage the beast, she conquered him with love, forgiveness, kindness, and understanding. Her true beauty is her inner beauty, and her ability to see my inner beauty. Ignoring all the times I yelled at her, said bad things, pushed her away, and hated her. She stood firm and believed one day the beast would go away. What a truly amazing woman. Now I sleep on her couch, and grow and heal every day.

Two weeks passed, and we seemed to fall back into our old relationship patterns. She would whine, yell, and nag, and I would start to yell back. But this time was different because halfway through I would simply hold my tongue and just agree with her. This was a great diffusing method; by not engaging I took out her fire, disabled her. She would walk away satisfied that she made her point, and most of all that I heard her. So I felt she needed a break, and decided to go up to my farm in Northern California for a few days. I drove my Porsche up there, and it was amazing on gas mileage. I made it from San Diego to Sacramento on one tank of gas. When I got to the farm it was just another beautiful day in the country. Ross, my ranch hand at the time, was feeling a little uneasy about the farm, and he had an awkward energy. The bathroom was still unfinished, and had been out of use for two months due to a remodel, and a hard time finding laborers up there. You can't rely on these country people to show up. So I asked Bill, my grower from that area, if he could recommend a tile guy. He gave me Eric. Eric and I hit it off right away, and Ross took off to San Diego for his grandma's funeral. That night, Eric and I talked about what had just happened to me at my house in San Diego; the attempted robbery, being tased, etc. I was warning him to keep an eye out on the farm just in case. We had a few beers, and Eric mentioned how my life sounded so much like a movie. Eric decided to stay the night for safety reasons, and although I didn't really know him, it comforted me to have someone to stay with me at the house. In the next three days Eric and I really connected and became close. We understood each other and realized we could help each other out. Eric had a lot of knowledge about farming, cultivating marijuana. When I learned of his experience and expertise in cultivation we started discussing him becoming a ranch hand on my farm. On the third night, Eric and I were talking when Eric heard someone yelling at the front gate. It was around 10:30 pm. We could see the headlights. Eric turned, looked at me, and asked, "Are you expecting anyone?" I was definitely not. I was shocked that someone would show up in the darkness of the country. So I grabbed the machete by the door, and walked outside to see who it was, to face my fear. Eric came from behind with a big stick and said, "This is how we do it in the country, we stick together to confront our problems." Again, he made me feel safe, and I realized I could trust this guy. Here he was sticking his neck out for me after meeting me only three days ago. We approached the headlights, when I heard a familiar voice: "Daveed Daveed, it's Juan from Covalo." "Oh shit Juan, what are you doing here?" It was Juan, my grower, from Mendicino Valley.

He laughed when he saw the big stick and machete, and he joked it was a good thing we didn't have guns. We welcomed him into the house. Juan had come up with his brother from Mexico looking to buy land in Yuba county. It was strange that he had picked that day. That night we spoke about what happened to me in San Diego, and Juan sat shocked and amazed. The next morning we went out for breakfast, and I showed Juan a few properties. I had to leave for San Diego at 1 pm. Still feeling my ex-wife needed some space, I called my friend Cat. Cat was an ex-girlfriend of mine that I had known for over 20 years, and remained friends with off and on. She had a one-bedroom apartment in Del Mar with an ocean view. Cat and I dated in our early twenties, so we knew each other for quite some time. Cat was a very peculiar creature. She had an inventive mind, but no follow through. She was always looking for the next big thing, or trying to chase rich guys. But the more she tried to chase the rich guys, the older and unhappier she became. That night Cat invited me over for dinner. She was making seared scallops as an appetizer and fish tacos for dinner. We opened some wine, and began reminiscing about the past. Cat had always been in love with me, and asked me several times to think about marrying her. She was a great cook, kept the house well, but I just wasn't sexually attracted to her. She asked me why I was limping, and she could tell my body was sore. So after a few glasses of wine, we began to relax and I told her the truth about my recent life. These stories seemed to excite her and make her nervous all at the same time. She began to tell me that she feared for my safety and made me promise to ensure no one followed me home. I assured her that I was making all efforts to know that people were not following me. We finished dinner and opened a second bottle of wine, and Cat asked me to stay the night. I accepted and felt relieved that I could finally rest.

My life was changing every minute; I was changing every second. At this time, I was still in full swing in the medical marijuana business. My farm was starting to produce a monthly income, My warehouse was on track producing an income every three weeks. Money was not a problem. I still had all my contacts and business was good. When Morning came, and Cat suggested I move in with her. She even had a curly haired dog she named David, which I found really odd. She said if she couldn't have the real me, she at least had a David. Cat's house was a nice break, and I knew no one would know I was there. I felt safe. Cat and my relationship was always a little rocky. Even though she seemed to care, she had a dark side. So when she asked me to move in, I knew she would change her mind as quickly as she made it. With Cat, it was always about how she could benefit. We started having sex, and after a few days she woke up one morning, and said it wasn't going to work anymore. My feelings were right about her. So I packed up my things to stay at the farm for a few days. I didn't want to stay at any one location for too long. So this moving actually made me feel safe. I would even borrow cars from my friend Tony every other week to throw people off my trail. Little did I know the DEA had been following me all along.

Chapter 5: The Grim Reaper and the DEA

By the third day at the farm I got a call from Cat asking when I was coming back. She had changed her mind again. So I flew back to have a chat with Cat. We spoke for a long time, and decided I would stay with her for a month. I would contribute money towards food; I offered to pay rent, but she refused. I felt I needed to stay with Cat, and not my ex-wife, for the safety of my children. I thought by moving around no one could trace me. Plus, my ex-wife was scared that the armed robbers still might be after me. Some nights I would get a hotel, some nights I would stay at Cat's, some nights at my farm. Even though I was moving so much, I still had the fear that whoever sent those people knew me, and their intentions were bad. I knew I needed to change my life. But I was still in the dark energy of the medical marijuana business. My ex-wife would call me to see if I was coming by to stay the night. I didn't want to go to her home, but to hear the joy in her voice when she heard mine brought me happiness, so I didn't mind. I couldn't figure out what was happening to me. Meanwhile, Cat and I were on a rollercoaster. One day she wanted me to move in, the next day she was angry and asking me to move out. I knew in my heart this wasn't going to work out, so I started to look for my own apartment. It took three weeks, but I found a place in Del Mar with an ocean view. It was $3000 a month with SDG&E, water, and cable. I put down my deposit but the landlord said there would be a month delay. So I drove up to my farm to pick up a few pounds of medical Marijuana and check in.

The drive up takes 9.5 hours, but it was fun driving my Porsche. I met up with Eric, took care of some business, and drove home the next day. On the drive home I kept thinking about how I was homeless and angry that my life was in shambles. Three and half hours into my drive I hit a traffic jam. There was a fire on highway 5. I was stuck in a standstill for three to four hours. I started making phone calls handling business, which made me even more angry. Then Juan called and said he gave away a pound of medical marijuana to someone because I owed them and I almost blew my lid. In that very moment I felt my right leg (calf) tighten up. I didn't really think anything was wrong, and I remained on the phone for another hour. I was yelling a lot, but I fixed the money issue. After I hung up the phone my leg felt tighter. I had been in traffic for seven hours and had six more left of the drive. I pulled over to gas up and get lunch from In and Out Burger and stretch my leg. My right leg was very tight and uncomfortable. But my mind was on the issues I was dealing with on the phone. I continued on my journey home. My leg was now very uncomfortable. I was visualizing the last two months of my life. I began to realize how much stress I had been under from being tased, tearing my knee ligament, the attempted robbery, moving, losing my grower, finding Eric, living with my ex-wife, staying with Cat, and now losing money because my "friends" were giving it away. No wonder I had a tight leg. By the time I got to L.A. with two hours left of driving, I knew in my heart I had a blood clot. I pulled into San Diego and went to my warehouse first. I dropped off the pounds of product I got from the farm, and drank a six-pack of beer with Mike, my grower, to wash down that thirteen-hour drive, and calm my nerves. It was now the middle of April. Mike and I had made a plan for the next month's grow. One room was coming up at the end of April, the second room was coming up the second week of May, and the third room was coming up the end of May. We were going to be stocked up, and all of our hard work from last year was now going to pay off. The farm was also at full swing, and Eric's expertise was keeping everything on track, healthy, and abundant. Even though I was homeless, I was still secure in knowing I had money coming in from my warehouse and my farm. After leaving Mike at the warehouse I drove over to my ex-wife's house. I walked in and she asked what was wrong with my leg, and why I was limping. I explained that I felt like I had another blood clot. She asked me why and I told her that my calf was tight and it hurt to walk on it. She gave me an Aspirin and elevated my leg. I relaxed and had a cold beer. I was glad to be at her house. She asked if I wanted to go to the hospital that night, and I said no. The next day I woke up and the swelling had gone down, and I could walk normally. I second-guessed that it was a blood clot and decided to go to work. Within four hours of work my right leg started to tighten up and swell. It stiffened up and I knew I had been right the first time. Later that day I went home to rest. When my ex-wife came home I asked her to book me an appointment for the next morning. Blood clots are very serious and deadly. If it dislodged and travelled, it would have killed me. But I insisted on waiting until morning. 8 am I was in the doctor's office that my ex-wife works in. Again my swelling had gone down, and the doctor looked at my leg. "There is no visual evidence of a blood clot," he said, but I insisted there was something wrong. I did have a DVT five years earlier on a plane. It was the same circumstances; lots of stress and injuries. I knew how blood clots felt. It is very painful and uncomfortable. The doctor recommended I take Xerelleto, an anti-coagulant, just in case. This would protect me from clots and work right away. So I took the meds and off to work I went. Around 11 am my ex-wife informed me that I had an ultrasound appointment at 3 pm. So I finished work at 2:30 and made it to my appointment. The ultrasound operator was a friendly guy and made small talk. He looked at my leg and said there were no signs of clots. He lubed up my right leg, ran the ultrasound over it, and immediately I heard the first click. The first clot was inches away from my main artery. Then a few inches more, a second click. Then by the top of my knee, where I tore my ligament, another click. Then another click as he reached my calf. Then a cluster of clots in my lower calf. He turned ghost white. I turned and looked at him, and asked, "What are all those clicks?" He said each one is a blood clot, and asked who my doctor could possibly be. He said I needed to go to the emergency room right away. I was in awe. He even said he had never seen so many clots in one person. That day the grim reaper was yet again knocking on my door. The ultrasound guy finally got my doctor on the phone and told him how much of an emergency this was. The doctor said I would be fine due to the anticoagulant medicine I had taken earlier. I asked the ultrasound guy for the phone, "Are you sure Doc, I want to be around tomorrow." He said yes so I ended my appointment and went home to rest. By now my leg was hard as a rock, and really hurt. I was so glad I went to the doctor's that day. Two clots had passed my right knee, and were heading for my main artery. One was six inches away, and that could have been the end. The Grim reaper was knocking at my door! This was a true turning point in my life. I realized that your body creates health issues according to the level of stress you are under and what you hold onto. What you store in your body comes out in disease; clots, heart attacks, cancer, etc. I was close to death. When you see your life flash before your eyes, you perceive life differently. That day my eyes changed. My heart changed. I saw my ex-wife in a whole new light. She was no longer annoying. Her voice became beautiful. Her eyes saw through me. That day she became my closest and best friend again. I found myself appreciating her, and being so thankful she was by my side. That day I gained admiration and respect for the woman I had ignored for eighteen years. I was truly grateful. My heart now feels good, and the blood clots are gone. The first week was tough. I laid on the couch and didn't work. I was still in the marijuana business. But I was so focused on this newfound relationship, after having the clots I decided to just stay with my ex-wife. Now her house felt like home. My body, mind, and soul was going through such turmoil, but having her there gave me a sense of security. Even with all this change we had tense moments. We still got in arguments, but at least I had become aware of what was happening between us. I was now appreciative, whereas before I took her for granted. I now considered her feelings, whereas before I expected. This year has been a tremendous blow to my soul. Once again I found myself in trouble with the law; not only had I been tased seven times in the first week of February, faced an attempted armed robbery in the second week of February, moved out of my beach house, lived with my ex-wife for a few days, learned to forgive her, made amends, lived in and out of hotels, stayed with friends, lived at the farm, drove back only to find out I had six potentially deadly blood clots, it wasn't over yet.

It was May 1. My day started as many others, I woke up at 6:30 am, and started packing up my medical marijuana to get it ready for the day's meeting with Javier's niece who I had never met before. My ex-wife would have flipped. She was adamant when I moved in about not having medical marijuana around the kids. Javier had requested 50 pounds of top grade marijuana, a pound of honey oil, and a pound of wax. This made me very nervous, as it was a huge order. Javier was a new client, but was referred to me by a reliable source (or so I thought). Bill, my friend and grower, from northern California, was supposed to meet me at 9 am that morning, and then I was going to meet Javier's niece at 10:30 am. Bill was bringing me my product from my farm; roughly ten pounds of indoor and some wax. At 8 am I rang Bill, who said he was passing through L.A. and would be in my area around 9:30 am. This was perfect timing. Then I rang Javier's niece, and there was no answer. I packed up Javier's order, but made it 25 pounds of chronic indoor, valued at $84,000, knowing that the order of 50 would be too much risk. Meanwhile, Bill kept texting me asking if I had the $8,000 I owed him. I told him yes and I would give it to him as soon as he arrived. 9:30am came and Bill was not picking up his phone. I texted him a few more times but there was no response. Then Javier's niece called and confirmed our 10:30am meeting at the Broken Yolk restaurant in Mission Valley. I asked her to meet me inside so we could exchange paperwork and cash. She refused and said she could just meet outside in the parking lot. This made me feel very uncomfortable, and I should have just trusted my instinct. $84K was a lot to trust in a parking lot, and in this business a lot could go wrong. It attracts a lot of low characters, and a lot of people are out to rob you, as I already learned. I already had a bad feeling about Javier, and now I was having a bad feeling about his niece. I don't know why I went against my gut that day, but I did. As I pulled into the Broken Yolk, I called Javier's niece, and asked her what kind of car she was driving. She said a big F250 grey color. As I pulled up, I had butterflies in my stomach. I knew something was wrong. There she was waiting. I parked my Porsche, and got out to meet her. Then she rudely asked if I had brought her product, and if she could see it. Right then my stomach sank. I knew in my heart something was wrong. I opened up the back of my trunk to show her a duffel bag with ten pounds of marijuana in it, when out of nowhere at least ten DEA cars pulled up on me. Everyone got out of their car with guns drawn and yelling "Freeze! Get on the ground! Do not move. Stretch your hands up and your legs out wide." That was it. I knew I had been set up, and my career in the medical marijuana business had been changed forever. I was in awe. Shocked yet calm. My mind was spinning, and the lady that was supposed to be Javier's niece had run off. Realizing she was part of the sting, I laid on the ground as the DEA handcuffed me. Personally, I did not feel I was breaking any laws. Medical marijuana is a senseless prosecution for the DEA to waste their time on. I was shocked they had so many men there. But there I was handcuffed, watching them search my Porsche. I immediately asked to speak to my attorney, but they said it would be a while. I told them I had my medical marijuana card and a collective paper, but they didn't care, they were federal. They proceeded to ask me more questions, and I once again asked to contact my attorney. They refused. Asking if I was under arrest the DEA just stated that we would talk about that later. Then the top DEA agent came over and introduced himself. He said they had been watching me for a few months, and they had knowledge of my warehouse, and had two search warrants; one for my warehouse and one for my ex-wife's house where I had been staying. The head DEA agent requested the keys to my warehouse and my ex-wife's house. He said to either give him the keys or be responsible for the cost to break down the doors at both locations. "If you cooperate with us, we won't do any damage. If you don't we will break down the doors...and how would your ex-wife feel about her door being busted open?" He chuckled. He asked if I had any weapons, booby traps, or guard dogs. I replied no, and nothing was at my ex-wife's house. They had me handcuffed at the Broken Yolk parking lot while they sent agents to my ex-wife's house and my warehouse. My life was flashing before my eyes. There I was at 48 busted by the DEA, watching them take $84K in medical marijuana, my new Porsche, my cash, and now I was losing my warehouse (another quarter million plus). My life had changed in an instant. I was numb in disbelief. My luck had run out. I just had to surrender and flow with what was happening to me. Now I would have to move out of my ex-wife's house or I was going to jail. Before getting into the medical marijuana business, I always realized there was a chance of this happening, but I didn't really realize the effect it would have on me, my ex-wife, and my two sons. I felt like a failure. I couldn't believe my life. I was just going to have enough money to purchase a house, get back on my feet from the bankruptcy from 2008-2012 when the recession hit and real estate took a tank. Now I had nothing, absolutely nothing. Then the DEA loaded me up in their SUV and drove me off to my ex-wife's house. Again they refused to let me speak to my attorney. As we drove there we talked a little bit about how I got into the medical marijuana business, and I explained after the 2008-2012 recession I lost everything. I closed my business in 2012 after the disastrous trip to Hawaii, and started my medical marijuana business. The DEA was acting like they were my friends but all along they were trying to get information from me. They used small talk and special psychology techniques to engage with me to extract information. As we got to my ex-wife's house I was in disbelief at how many DEA agents were there. The DEA must have thought they were onto something bigger. Their search warrant was for honey oil, wax, butane, but I had none of these things. As soon as I entered my ex-wife's house they un-cuffed me and asked me to sit down on the couch while they completed a search of the home. Still in disbelief, I started to communicate with the agents. They stated how calm I was, and how well I was taking this. Yes, I was calm on the outside, but on the inside I was sad, depressed, and angry. There wasn't much I could do, and making a scene would only make things worse. All I could do was make light of a horrible situation. I had to find the good in the negative that was happening to me. I knew my life had changed forever. After they searched my ex-wife's house they started to question me, and I again asked for my attorney. The head agent simply stated, "We'll talk about that later." Then they found a safe in my ex-wife's room, and asked for the code. I explained it wasn't mine, and we called her for the combination. Luckily she picked up the phone, and the head agent explained to her that they needed the combination to the safe or they would break it open. She immediately left work and came home. As we were waiting for the arrival of my ex-wife, the DEA agents questioned me, arrested me, handcuffed me, and when my ex-wife finally came home, began to escort me to the car. As I passed her, I told her to say hello to my new friends. And off to jail I went. Wow, I really couldn't believe my world came crashing down so fast. The severity of what happened did not really sink in until I landed in jail. That really is where the scum of the earth is. Mostly drug addicts, DUIs, people who have committed crimes to supply their habits. I could see America truly has a drug problem. Numerous repeat offenders on a daily crash course with the law. My legs started to swell up from my blood clots, and I requested my medication. They refused because it was a sample not a prescription. So I called bail bonds and started the bail process. My bail was set at $35,000. This was not a good day for me. They asked me how I was going to pay and I said I had cash in the bank. So they sent down a representative to meet me in jail in person, which took a few hours, but I was happy to be out of that hell hole and in a room by myself. The representative finally made it down, and we were able to talk through the glass window. He said I looked credible, and he was going to authorize my bail without a cosigner, and since I was paying cash he was going to give me a discount. I agreed, went back to my cell, and waited to be bailed out. The bail bond man said it would be a few hours, but it took over 24. I called my ex-wife and once again she was behind me 100%. What a truly amazing woman; through all my hardship she was behind me. She was holding my head up above water as I sank. She did tell me I would have to move out, and she didn't want the medical medical marijuana around our boys. I finally understood. I realized what I had just gone through in the last three months; almost dying three times. I had been living a risky life. Boy, I did not see that coming...being set up by my "friends" and robbed by the DEA...they took everything. I was left with my shorts shirt and flip flops!

Chapter 6: Making Peace With My Father

I find myself starting over at 48. I am looking within to find my peace. My daily yoga class has been my saving grace. When all else fails, I look for a yoga class to heal my mind, my soul, and my body. I reflect back on my life, and it's been pretty adventurous. I took a lot of risks, gained a lot, and lost it all. But one thing has been consistent through my most difficult times in life, and that is my ex-wife's support. Now as I look into her eyes, I see peace. Sure we still have our moments, but now I understand her. Now I know to listen to her tone, and watch her body movements. I see the expressions on her face. I listen instead of react. I hear her needs and let go of mine. I share my feelings, and explore new territory of emotions with the mother of my children. It reminds me of when our children were first born; I could tell by the pitch of their cry if they were hungry, scared, needed to be changed, or simply needed to be held. She used to get so frustrated when I would hear our children cry, and I would let her know what they needed. She would say, "I am the mother, how would you know?" And I would simply reply, "I listen to their tone." Our eyes aren't the only things that see. Once you start looking within your true self, you start to see people differently. You open your heart even when you feel someone has wronged you, rid the past of the pain, and see the truth, which is always one-sided. To forgive is divine. To hold onto anger and hate is poison to the mind, body, and soul. It took me losing everything to open my eyes and see the beauty in my ex-wife. To learn to appreciate her when my world went dark. She was the one who opened the door, and shined some light on me. She warmed my heart, and I learned to appreciate. I learned to be grateful, and I learned to open my heart, my ears, and my eyes. What I thought before was only my selfish anger. I clearly did not understand her dramatization. I always felt she was acting. Matter of fact, when we first met at my salon she used to run around saying, "I'm an actress, I'm an actress." And I would tell her, "Great, well act like a receptionist, because that's your job." But every time we got into a fight, I seemed to lose. She knew how to push my buttons and pull my triggers. She is very manipulative. I would become angry, lonely, and frustrated. The more I cursed this woman, the worse my life became. Now at 48, I seek peace, love, and forgiveness. Today I am truly a man. Unselfish, kind, learning, appreciative, and grateful to be alive. We all seek the materials in life, but few seek internal beauty. After losing everything, I realized that inner peace is the most important treasure anyone can have. And that's why this book is important. Material things come and go, but inner peace is a blessing. Now I looked to mend my family relationships. Looking within, I realized I was angry. I did push people away. So I realized I must take the first step, and drove up to my father's house to give him the respect of being his son.

On August 2nd I asked my ex-wife to come with me to Paso Robles California, since she had been a big part of the new healing in my life. I invited her to help me show my family that amends were possible, and that I did see things differently. To have her on my side to help me heal, and move forward in my life. She picked me up when I had fallen and shined her heart of love onto me. She instilled hope, and through all the years of me pushing her away she has been there waiting to be my friend. She told me, "I have always been your friend, you just haven't seen it." I guess she was right, and had been right all along. My best friend has always been in front of me. It's like the story of the alchemist; we are all looking for the pot of gold, searching the end of rainbows, but when you get there, it usually disappears into the mist. The truth is, the pot of gold is always right in front of you, if you open your eyes to see the gold inside of the people that surround you. I realize now that the fun of life is being around people who you love and who love you. It took me 48 years to open my eyes. To allow people to be near me. To understand their needs, and not just mine. That weekend was a big journey home for me. To open my heart, and ask for forgiveness from my father and brother, and accept their reaction, whatever it may be. To at least take the first step in healing this long-standing family feud. To acknowledge their feelings, forgiving them, forgiving myself, and to let go of the anger to free my soul, and expect nothing but grace. By me taking the first step, I have grown as a man. Now I realize that making amends, and forgiving my ex-wife is the key to letting go of the beast. I have my days of depression awaiting my trail date. My whole life has changed, in a weird and fantastic way. I am at peace. And my new best friend opened up that door for me. I hope people can learn from my mistakes, from my anger and my love. How I opened my heart, which in turn opened my eyes to my true self. It taught me to share my emotions, to forgive and forget, to simply let go. Renewing myself and everything around me. We as humans are afraid of change, but the only thing that is consistent in life is daily change. Time heals, they say, but I believe it is the ability to open your heart, your mind, and let go of what you are holding onto. We tend to get our feelings hurt, and in our minds we use that emotion as a wedge in our life. I just realized that I myself have lived this way for many years. My new path is to make peace with myself. To make peace with my ex-wife, and my two teenage sons. To make peace with my father, my brother, and my sister. This year I have learned a lot. I have risked a lot. And lost a lot. But in the midst of all this negativity, I have found myself. I have found a gift of harmony, I have made amends with my ex-wife, but most importantly I now appreciate her. I have learned to let go of the past, stay in the present moment, and work on healing myself. I await a trial on twelve Felony counts of sales of marijuana, transportation, and cultivation, and the grey area of my life in the medical marijuana business went black. My ex-wife has proved to be my guardian angel. I'm now looking to change my life. I am back in the hair business; starting a new life from the bottom. I just completed yoga teacher training, which really helped me find peace and allowed me to let things go. Each day my friendship with my ex-wife becomes more beautiful. I see her for her true self; a person full of compassion for others. Love tends to bring out the worst and best in people. All along that's what happened to us. We were both in love, and the turmoil of our marriage, kids, new businesses, buying a new home, and two new cars ultimately got to us. We did not learn to grow together. Yet through thick and thin my ex-wife has always been there with her love, support, and honest opinion. I have learned to forgive her through the force of my actions. When all others left my side, and my anger pushed people away, she was there. Now we hug each other, and tell one another how much we love each other. I look forward to seeing her, and having her around. I enjoy her companionship. I enjoy her two little dogs, and her new little bunny. I enjoy having conversations with her. I understand a little bit more about her each day. It grows. Some days we revert back, but we both know our triggers, and are open to communicating better. We take the time to learn about each other. We are more considerate to each other, and we now try to help each other. If only I knew this 18 years ago. If I only knew to compromise, to listen, to care, and to understand. All I have to do is acknowledge, not engage or react. To be there to help instead of fight. To love not to expect. To appreciate and forgive, instead of being angry and taking. To understand and flow. I guess that is the hardest thing was to let go of my ego, and be man enough to open my heart and feel emotions. To share my feelings, and to hold and nurture the mother of my children. To see life differently. I now have the chance to make the second half of my life better than the first. I now have to face the consequences of my actions. I must improve my perception to see the light instead of the darkness. I must step out of my comfort zone. To go beyond my means, to the unexpected. I continue to educate myself, improve my harmony, and help those around me.

I was very glad my ex-wife had chosen to come with me to make amends with my father. Her support alone was comforting. She, her two dogs, and the bunny all came for the ride. My father's last text to me has been, "Have a nice life." It hurt me so much I became angry and explosive. I was already having problems with my brother, my sister, and now my father? What type of example was I setting for my kids? My oldest son, 18 years of age, was being a typical rebellious teenager, trying to find his path in this world. He resented me. He would spend time with his cousins, my father, and my brother, but he wouldn't talk to me. At least I realized all this would pass in time. To be humbly waiting patiently is how I had to rebuild my life. I had to let go of the turmoil of the past to renew my relationship with my sons. I saw my younger son being influenced by his older brother. They could not see the pain of family dynamics. So as a man, I simply had to let go of how I felt someone had wronged me. I had to accept where I was with my torn up relationships with my family. To show my children change is possible. I look back on how important these relationships are, and the true depth and beauty of having your mother and father in your life. To sit down at dinner, laugh about past experiences, to cry and surrender. I need to amend current mistakes, and improve the words that we exchange. I want to feel the warmth of family once again. I am willing to surrender and admit I was wrong, I was angry and blind at my father for what he had last texted me (Have a nice life!). On the drive up my ex-wife and I discussed how things may turn out with my father. My mother knew I was coming but I asked her not to tell my father. Because of his stubbornness I knew he wouldn't be interested in seeing me. I knew I had to surprise him to meet him face to face, and show him I am truly sorry. Turns out I was glad my ex brought those dogs and even the little bunny, they too seemed to support and love me. I was playing our meeting in my mind over and over. What would I say? How would he react? We both had such deep wounds and wedges between us. Both of my children were already in Paso, and had just done a 28 mile hiking trip with my dad. I would have loved to have been on that camping trip. I was the only one missing out on family functions. Even my own kids got to go up and spend time with them.

Rolling into Paso, our gas tank was on reserve, but I told her that we could make it. She got nervous, feeling like I was taking yet another risk. Luckily, we made it to Paso on fumes. We went to the hotel she booked for us, located in the ghetto, right behind the old projects. We got into a fight trying to check in, and I had to bite my tongue to maintain the peace. We realized we weren't even at the right hotel, and found another one that was dog friendly. The whole time she kept telling me I didn't need to be so angry and explosive. I appreciated this, but told her to respect me and try to help the cause. We both calmed down and drove to La Quenta. I was glad to be leaving that ghetto hotel. We stopped and got gas, and I was pleased to see La Quenta was a bright yellow, shiny hotel located in the wineries of Paso Robles. I loved the openness and the location. The colors cheered me up. I knew this was the perfect spot. This was a sign of good karma. My ex-wife checked us in, and was happy. She said we were in a newer suite, and it was only three weeks old. She then sneakily said she didn't notify the front desk about the dogs or the bunny. We looked around and saw other people with dogs, so we knew it was dog friendly. Immediately she loved our two-bedroom suite. It was nice, clean, upscale, with a balcony. I unloaded her belongings out of the car while she got the animals organized in the room. Paso was a hot dry 105 degrees that typical day. It reminded me of why I left. So I changed into my shorts, jumped in the pool, and enjoyed washing off the five-hour drive. I stayed at the pool for 45 minutes to cool down and give My ex-wife some space. As I returned to the room she asked if I would go get her a glass of wine. So I checked the hotel wine room and the cheapest bottle was $35. I told her I would run to the store, pick up some cheese and crackers, and pick up a bottle of wine for us. On my way to the store I called my mother to see where my dad was, and she said he was home. I drove past the store since it was on the way to my parents' house, and decided it was the perfect moment to face my father alone. My mother didn't know that as I spoke to her on the phone I was driving towards her house. She was trying to say it would be better to stop by the next day, attempting to stall the meeting altogether. I told her I would be pulling into the driveway any second. She was happy, surprised, and cautious all at once. Driving into their driveway brought back a rush of childhood memories. I could see the new front yard that I helped pay for and install four years ago. I was proud of the beauty it brought to the front of their house. I could see my dad had let the land go a little. The weeds were six feet high on the sides of the house, and the back yard was a mess. Two and a half acres is a lot of land to maintain as you're getting older. I parked my car and was very happy to be there. I felt nervous and sad that I had missed all that time not seeing my dad, and in turn, my mother. I approached the front door, noticing the beautiful plants I had planted in the front yard; they were overgrowing but bursting with life. It was like they were dancing to see me. Knocking on the front door I could hear my mother and father talking. I waited a few minutes, still heard them talking, and decided to just open the door and walk in. My mom was standing in the kitchen, and I saw my father organize something on the living room floor. I said hello to my mother, and immediately walked to my father with open arms. I said, "Hello Dad, I am sorry." He stood up, I approached him, and I just gave him a big hug. He was resistant at first and said he was still mad, and it would take some time to heal (still being my stubborn dad). He asked me what I was doing up here, and I responded, "I came to see you dad. To make peace and give you the respect of being my father." We were both crying. "I am sorry for the things I said to you. I never should have said them. I was hurt and emotionally devastated. That is why I exploded and attacked you. But I realize now how wrong I have been and how important you are in my life. I came to make peace with you, and ask for your forgiveness." Seeing my father made me realize that life is short. He had shrunk six inches. His health was dwindling, and my time was limited for both of our sakes. I saw how difficult it was for him to get up off the floor. He looked old, and all the years of not taking care of his body had caught up to him. No longer did he look like the strong father I knew. He now resembled a frail old man, on his last journey in life. It broke my heart to see him this way. I held him in my arms, and it warmed my heart to make peace before he was gone for good. We both wept tears of pain, and sorrow, and joy. As we let each other go, I said, "I miss you dad, and I love you. I need you in my life, and you are important to me." He started to resist again, when something changed in him. He looked up at me and said, "I'm glad you're here son, it's been a long time since we spoke." I gave him another hug, said I am sorry again, and we both cried holding each other. I then walked over to my mother who was so apparently happy for the peace between us. As she cried, I gave her a big hug and told her I loved her. My heart felt so much better; this was definitely the right thing to do. To make amends for all the pain, frustration, and hurt I caused my father, and in turn my mother. As we all wiped our eyes, we began to talk. I was surprised how open and receptive my father was being. We talked about the last few years, and I told him I had almost gotten killed three times, and how it made me realize that the most important things in life are family and love. How the most important thing in my life was to make amends with him. It was a great day; it was a Sunday I'll never forget. The more we talked, the happier my mother got, and the warmer my father became. I knew I was making progress. I realized that peace had been made. He thanked me for the all expensive gifts I had given him throughout the years: trips to Hawaii, fishing in Oregon, loaning him $50,000 to fix up his house, a new truck...I told him he was welcome, and it was a pleasure to help him back then when he needed it and I was doing well. He said, "You are the only one of my kids that has gone out of their way to help me. To just give me things." I thanked him for finally acknowledging that, and told him how important it was for me to hear that from him. We both needed this day to heal. It was such a great feeling to be able to speak to my father again. The things that used to bother me about him no longer affected me. I was grateful to be there in his house talking to him and hugging him. I didn't even realize a few hours had passed by. I asked them if they had plans for dinner. Immediately my father perked up and said they would love to join us for dinner. Then I knew deep down he had forgiven me. I was very happy, my heart felt so open and warm. He looked at me and said, "Thank you son for coming up here. Now I can die in peace." I told him that I loved him and I told them both My ex-wife and I would be waiting at the restaurant for them. I had a warm glow about me as I got in the car. Tears of joy were rolling down my face. This was one of those life moments most people just pass by. Most people are too stubborn to admit they are wrong, and forgive and renew. I called my ex-wife and she was a little upset. I had been gone for two and a half hours. I explained what had happened, and that I made peace with my father. I told her how wonderful it felt to see him again, and how having him there was so important. She was so elated because she knew how important this was to me. She said she was honored to be a part of it. I thanked her for being a part of my family.

Before my parents arrived my ex-wife and I started to

argue. She brought up Hawaii and said the whole trip was my fault, and that my anger affected my relationship with my sons. I looked at her and realized she had drunk that whole bottle of wine. Alcohol tends to trigger her emotions, and she reverts back to our old relationship patterns. As I was getting irritated, I realized where this conversation was headed. I stated, "I think we need to talk about this sober and at another time." Right then my parents showed up. She and I quickly changed our mood, excited that my father would be joining us for dinner. After four long years, we could speak freely with no guards up. This was an amazing gift to my mother. Both she and my ex-wife were glowing with joy to see me and my father getting along and communicating. This was a great gift for all of us. I really do love my father, and all these years had emotionally, physically, and mentally made me ill. This new connection was exactly what I needed at this point in my life. With all of the other turmoil I was facing, I knew I had to make peace for my health, my peace of mind, and to teach my children that forgiveness is possible. We had such a great time at dinner, I didn't want the night to end. The connection the four of us had that night was warm, loving, honest, and heartfelt. This was one of the greatest moments in my relationship with my father. We finished dinner, and I shared cheesecake with my ex-wife. My mother enjoyed the mud pie. We parted ways and my ex-wife and I were both elated. I knew just showing up and following my heart would be the key to opening up his heart. After dinner we all met at my parents' house. Having my ex-wife there made it a warm family experience. Watching her walk around my parent's house made me realize why I invited her on this journey; to mend my family. She was a big part of my life. She added warm love and enthusiasm to a tense situation. She and my father always got along, and I knew she would soften the mood. I was right, it was working like a charm. Around 11 pm my ex-wife and I started to head back towards our hotel. I was excited about this day; it was a major accomplishment. It felt so good to release the anger I had held inside me for so many years. To sit and watch my father in the twilight of his life, I knew in my heart this was truly a great day. It was wonderful to be reconnected with my father. Back at the hotel we went right to bed. My mind was spinning, and I couldn't believe this was real. I was so proud of myself for completely surrendering to my father. Morning came and Paso was heating up. I decided to stop by my brother Mike's house. We hadn't spoken in six years. He wasn't home, and it made me feel better that I at least made an effort. Not one time had my father, brother, or sister reached out to me since they had stopped speaking to me. We both needed to surrender and accept our actions. I saw the change in myself since I let go of the anger I felt for my ex-wife. I hoped to share this feeling with my siblings. But my whole time in Paso, I never saw my brother or my sister.

Chapter 7: My Darkest Days and Scooby Doo

After being robbed by the DEA I started to spiral down into an unaware deep depression. My life had crashed, and hard. Everything was taken out from underneath me. I was left with the shirt on my back, my shorts and flip flops (literally)! My source of income had dried up. My life was miserable. My heart was in pain. I didn't even have enough strength to get out of bed, but I did. Surrounded by darkness, I couldn't even feel my own heartbeat. It was as if the blood had stopped dry in my veins. The pain was like a knife slicing through my body. The realization of having lost everything was far worse than I had imagined. I knew I was taking a risk with my work, but I didn't realize the DEA would steal everything from me. They took my Porsche. They took my cash. They seized all my bank accounts. They set me up, and they took $84,000 in product. They cut down my warehouse, which was an estimated quarter million. They took my rent, my deposit, and even my ex-wife's child support. On May 1 I sat in a county jail numb to the world, awaiting my fate, and my new destination. Thinking back, I started to see all the mistakes I had made throughout my life. Each one came back as an open wound topped off with salt. It burned. My mind couldn't stop, and the pain would not go away. After 24 hours of being in a filthy cell with drug addicts and criminals I was released with a $35,000 bail. Luckily I was able to come up with 10% as an acceptable payment to the bails bondsman. Driving back to my ex-wife's house I still couldn't fully face the amount of pain I was in. I was excited to be released and freed. But signing all the paperwork with the bail bondsman made me realize I was in for a huge turn in my life. I needed to find my heart, my desire, and what really made me happy. Sure the medical marijuana business was fun, exciting, dangerous, and popular, but it also led to robberies, lie, and cheating. It was my "friend" who set me up on my fall from grace. Ultimately, I was the one who took the bait. My desire for money had surpassed my intuition and sense of right. I knew I was taking the risk; I just didn't think it would happen to me. After a few days, the numbness started to fade, and my ex-wife made it clear I had to leave. My children's eyes shined with great disappointment. The look on their faces said it all. I was a complete failure to them! I had nothing to my name. Even my ex-wife was disappointed in me. I was crushed. My mind kept getting darker and darker. It was difficult to face myself in the mirror. I looked old, tethered, and defeated. It was hard to speak with my own children. Only woe is me came out of my mouth. I was spitting vinegar. All my "friends" had turned their backs on me. I was truly alone in a miserable world of darkness. Sinking deeper and deeper into the hole. I was scratching the sides, trying to climb my way out, but I kept slipping deeper and deeper. May 6th I moved into my new apartment in Del Mar

California. This brought me a flashing moment of self-confidence. No longer was I sleeping on my ex-wife's couch. I now had my own place. A spark lived in me for a second. I had my friends Cory and Kane help me move into my place (I was still gun-shy from the robbery and DEA). My mind would race back to the robbery; who sent these guys? It was definitely someone I knew because the two girls had texted me three hours before the attack, which was their biggest mistake. I had read the texts and felt bad vibrations from the picture of the girl, and the words she used to text me. And sure enough, three hours later armed thugs were at my door. I was lucky to be alive. These thoughts were constantly passing through my mind. It was defeating me. I knew I had to change my life, and fast. I knew I could always do hair, and that is what I was best at. After moving to Del Mar I still had no car, so I began looking for work in a salon at Del Mar. I walked up and down the street, peeping into every little salon. Most of them had an odd feel to them. Only one had met me with open arms. I could feel their warmth. But for the most part the city of Del Mar had a weird sleepy old click to it. Not only that, I didn't realize I was in a deep depression. It was written all over my face. My shoulders were hunched over; even my body language displayed my defeat. I had lost all my confidence, my ability to create was gone. I was in pain, excruciating pain. Yet each day from 9-12 I would get up and go searching for the right fit of the salon for me. I guess my opening line of "I just lost everything. I'm 48 and just starting over" wasn't that inviting to owners. They could look into my eyes and see defeat. They could hear the lack of confidence in my voice. They could smell the fear from my body. I still forced myself to keep interviewing. By now it was the end of May and not once had my children come to visit. I think they were still shocked and afraid of what had happened. There was something odd about my apartment in Del Mar. It was a dark, dreary, sad, and an old place. There seemed to be a musty air of mold. And even the furniture was pulled and torn. It seemed to have been there for ages. I couldn't pinpoint the feeling, and my depression kept getting deeper. I was lonely, sad, and afraid. I would call people I hadn't seen in years just to hear a familiar voice. Just someone to hear me whine. The more I tried to make the new apartment a home, the more stressed I seemed to get. I called my ex-wife and begged her to move back in with her and the kids. I explained that I was having a hard time finding a job; I had interviewed over 50 salons, and no one had hired me. I was in a whirlpool of pain and everyone around me could see it. My ex-wife refused and kept saying "Hang in there, eventually something will give, and eventually you will find something you will like." All I could see was pain, failure, uncertainty, and no future. I couldn't believe this was my life. Why was this my fate? Who did I wrong to be crushed so hard? I really started to look within to see how I treated other people, and why I had no friends in my life. Even my own kids were at a distance from me. They weren't sure of who their father really was. There I stood in Del Mar, a defeated and lonely man. My clients were my friends, and when they came over they would try to cheer me up. They all attested to the weird energy of the grounds, the darkness and dreariness of the apartment, and how old it seemed.

In June I met Julie, my ex-girlfriend, at my house to do her hair color and cut. She arrived to find my apartment surrounded by sheriffs and police officers. She called me immediately and asked if I was OK; I said yes and I was on my way. When I arrived, I could see cops everywhere. Their bright yellow tape was blocking the entrance to my parking spot. I knew something serious had happened. I was so relieved to know that they weren't there for me. I pulled up next to Julie's car and saw she was in shock. She asked if everything was going to be ok. I said yes and we started walking to my apartment. I could tell Julie was nervous and unsure of the situation at hand. I saw the apartment manager Mike with an anguished and frustrated look on his face. He was sitting behind the yellow tape in front of the parking structure. I knew right away that whatever had happened, Mike was part of it. I could tell from the lost look in his eyes. His face had a severe expression of pain. I could tell someone had died, been murdered, or committed suicide. I knew it was serious; there were more than ten detectives and sheriffs combing around my new apartment. I led Julie upstairs, and starting foiling her hair when I saw the white coroner's car pull up right next to Mike's spot, directly underneath my apartment. The energy of the complex became very dreary and dark. Mike was lost, and I could tell it was someone close to him. Julie and I were shaken up, but I tried to keep it normal by making dinner. I made fresh halibut, eggplant, and some delicious curry rice. She and I sat on the balcony as the sun was setting. There was a beautiful orange glaze over the ocean, with hints of yellow. Meanwhile all the police were running around doing their thing. It was amazing to see the beauty in all the confusion. Julie loved the meal. I shampooed her and gave her a beautiful haircut. She left and I knew she was still shaken up because she forgot to pay me. Then the darkness of night set in, along with the darkness of being alone and in a deep depression. Between that and the energy of a murder or suicide right beneath my apartment, it was overwhelming. I called my ex-wife to see if I could stay with her due to what had just happened. She was worried that it was someone after me. I assured her it wasn't and that we would be ok. I was just freaked out from this and needed to clear my head. That night I looked up at the sky. It was a full moon. I could feel the spirits of restlessness in the air. I had to beg my ex-wife to let me stay with her; I assured her it would only be one night. As I stayed there I could feel an unusual attitude from my son, Dante. He was now 18 and going through a lot of personal changes, and he was definitely not happy having me in his house. So I just kept to myself that night. I was already so depressed and the murder/suicide did not help warm my heart or my spirit. I knew that being at my ex-wife's house was helping me have some sense of family and escape that darkness that shrouded my apartment, my mind, and my life. I had a dark cloud over me, and I couldn't get it to leave. Being in the same house as my children at least gave me company and a feeling of belonging. Even seeing my ex-wife was better than being alone. Deeper and deeper my depression went.

The next day I moved back into my apartment, and even asked my ex-wife if I could borrow one of her dogs to keep me company, seeing as it was the one year anniversary of my beloved dog Scooby Doo III. Scooby had passed a year ago in July at the age of 14. She was a large furry smoky silver Akita. I had her since she was six weeks old; she was my light. Scooby was my heart and soul, she was my best friend, my wife, and my soul mate. At night she would sleep right next to me with her head on a pillow. As she crawled into bed, she would nudge up to me, raise her glance over her shoulders, grunt a few times to see if I heard her, and wait for me to put my arm around her to spoon her. She would always let out a big sigh of pleasure knowing that we were one. I loved this dog Scooby Doo with all my heart. She had many human characteristics about her. She was my angel, a gift from God. She always waited patiently at home for me with loving emotions and excitement. A truly amazing animal. Even now as I write this, my eyes tear up, my heart sinks low, and I miss the love of my life. To have someone in your life for 14 years and then gone overnight leaves a huge hole in your heart. I must have cried for two months after she died. Losing her changed me. I lost my heart. I could smell her around the house, and I was heartbroken. I was a car with no wheels; my engine was broken. I was just a human shell. There were times I would see a glimpse of her around the corner. I would say "Scooby Doo," and realizing she was dead, I would cry. Sobbing until I had no more tears, sobbing until the pain would leave, but it never really did. My heart had been torn out of my chest. And now one year later, I had lost even more in my life. I had no future. The pain just kept growing. I would call clients or friends over for a glass of wine just to have someone to talk to. When my clients came to my apartment I would ask them to stay a while if they could. I did not want to be alone. A few weeks went by and I found out that the police incident was a suicide: the apartment manager's ex-wife had sliced her own throat. The irony was that it had occurred in my parking spot right underneath my apartment. I could feel the energy change, and it made things even more depressing. Now I knew I had to leave that apartment. I had to change my life; I had to remove the dark energy. I just couldn't figure out how. I had to quit smoking medical marijuana and drinking alcohol. They both just brought me down lower, deeper and darker. I could tell people could see my energy as I went into job interviews for salons. They would say that they had a chair for full rent but no rates to start up. I could have taken the deal, but nothing felt right. I thought the salons were either too Mom-and-Popish or the egos in them were too off-putting. In retrospect it was my own lack of self-confidence that was defeating me. I thought moving into the apartment would help raise my confidence, but then I decided to get Scooby's ashes which I had left at the vets for over a year.

I thought having her next to me would help my depression. But it only hurt worse. I felt having her in my new apartment would bring me love, but it only brought my heart a deeper sorrow. The day I finally made it to the vet I was in a good mood. I walked in and asked to pick up Scooby Doo's ashes. I was greeted by a flamboyant veterinarian assistant, who proved to be the best person for me that day. His eyes opened wide and said he was there the day I brought in Scooby. He said it warmed his heart to know that Scooby Doo was finally going home. My heart sank, and I broke into a million pieces. I could see the true concern and warmth of this man. He truly cared, and that eased my pain, but simultaneously made me more sensitive. I was fine until he brought her out in a beautiful redwood box. I could feel the weight of her in the box. It was heavier than I remembered, or my heart had just dropped, or both. Everyone standing in the office immediately recognized my sorrow. My mood went from happy to sad to severe pain. I tried to hold it in, but the minute I stepped out the front door I burst into tears. I screamed out from the bottom of my heart, "Scooby Doo, I love you and I miss you." I released as much as I could. That few second walk to my car felt like an eternity. I wept like a child as I sat in the car holding Scooby in my lap. I started to talk to her as if she were still alive. I could feel her next to me. In my heart I knew that dog truly loved me as I truly loved her. As I took her back to the apartment all I could think about was how I needed to get out of there. The suicide was the catalyst and Scooby was the motivation. It was thirty days into living at that Del Mar apartment, and my rent was due. I went in and told the manager I wasn't able to pay rent, because the DEA had seized my accounts and taken everything from me. Mike was really cool about it, and suggested I continue to look for a job and place an ad for a roommate. Now I was looking for a job, a roommate, and looking for someone to take over the lease. Mike said he would give me at least a week or two to try and solve this problem. I knew I needed to move, to be around my kids. I knew that would further motivate me; I needed to be around my family, I needed a home. Once again I found myself seeking her house for warmth. After running a two-week ad for a new roommate, with no response, I put up an ad for a two bedroom for rent. Within a week I got a response from a couple moving from Santa Barbara to Del Mar. We instantly matched energy, and when they found out I was a hairstylist the woman flipped with excitement. They took the apartment, and within a week she became my first client at the new salon I was working at.

Now I had a job, and my apartment was rented out, which relieved a lot of stress. I was still without a car, although I was borrowing my friend's car. Yet again, I called my ex-wife for a space to re-establish my life. I explained to her that her child support payment was reduced to $300 a month, but if she let me stay there I would continue to pay $933. It would help her, me, and the children. I also explained that I needed to buy a car, and instead of paying $3000 to rent in Del Mar, I could stay with her and rebuild my clientele as a hairstylist. Realistically, I could have gone back to the medical marijuana business, but it really didn't make me happy. Not only that, now I was facing charges with the DEA. It really had been a hell of a year.

Chapter 8: Getting Up

My ex-wife played hardball until the very last day I had to move out of my apartment. I was ready to sleep in my buddy's car if I had to. This was a difficult time in my life; once being a successful hairdresser, owning millions of dollars in real estate, owning multiple businesses and now…facing the possibility of sleeping in a car. I called her one last time and explained the benefit for the whole family. She finally agreed and allowed me to move in. I was happy to have company again. I finally felt less lonely. Even though my children were being typical teenagers and refusing to speak to me, it was nice just being around other human beings. About the same time, my ex-wife allowed me to stay at her house, I found a job at a Salon at the Forum Shopping Center in Carlsbad. It was a little pretentious, There were 35 stylists, 5 male and 30 female stylists, all the male stylist got along, but the females stylist that worked there had a arrogant attitude as if there shit didn't stink! Most of them were very un-friendly, had their nose in the air, They would walk around saying I work in La Costa or I had worked in Beverly Hills. As if this made them better! But being the sarcastic person I am, I would ask them where do you live? Then they would respond Oceanside, vista or San Marcos. If you know north county San Diego these are the less affluent areas, They did not like the realization I had brought to their attention. but it was a high end mall, and it made me happy to drive to work every day. Finally, after two and a half months, things were looking up. I had a job, I had a place to live, a roof over my head, and a couch to sleep on. It was a start. I still had a few clients that I could work with at my little salon in Pacific Beach, California. So I had at least a few pennies in my pocket. But I was still struggling, and continuing my fall into a deep depression. It takes a lot of time to build up a clientele in the hair business. I still felt an unshakable black cloud hanging over my head. My oldest son and I would bump heads; I knew he resented me. What son doesn't resent his father at 18? I knew it was made worse by years of him being manipulated by his mother. She would constantly drill it into their heads, "See how your father treats me, you would think he would respect the mother of his children." I am still so upset about how this affected their impressionable minds. My oldest son would tell me, "Dad I don't like you because of the way you treat my Mom." How could I win against that? I tried to use this chance of living with him to rebuild our relationship. I could still cook for him, help him out, and slip him a few bucks. Every now and then he would talk to me. He wouldn't say much, but it was more than nothing at all. I was making ground, one small inch at a time. I was goldmining a new relationship with my son, picking away at the hardened dirt from years of compacting mental manipulation from his mother. Even though I had learned to greatly appreciate her for helping me in my time of need, and even though I forgave her and let things go, we still had this wedge that brought up issues: my son. I always tried to remember, life is short, and even shorter if you hold onto anger. Each day I would send him love, and each day he would try to push me away. I would go into his room and clean it up, make his bed, and do his laundry. But each time he would get angry at me for touching his stuff. I tried to explain that his mother wanted me to help keep the house clean, but this would just make things worse. Then one day my son spoke to me and asked, "Dad I need new tires, do you know anyone?" I simply said, "Yes." This was my chance to do something good for him. This was my chance to get to know him. This was the opening in the eclipse that was my son. "Yes Son, leave your car and I will make it happen." He argued with me, "Why do I need to leave my car with you?" He thought I was trying to borrow it. I explained I would take it in for him. He shrugged his shoulders and with a big sigh said, "Ok. I guess I can do that." I dropped him and Christopher off at school that day, and went on craigslist to find a pair of decent tires. I was on a budget, and I knew I couldn't afford much. Then I found a set of four used tires for $200; all four BF Goodrich in good shape. So I booked the tire appointment and drove down to have them installed. As the tire guy changed them, he found one of the old tires had a nail in it. Two of the old tires had very bad cracks. And the fourth was very worn down. I guess my son really needed tires after all. It made me feel better that I was able to help him, and keep him safe. The new tires even looked better. I made it home an hour late, and they had already walked home from school. My son said, "Thanks Dad," and drove off into the sunset. The next day his attitude had come back. He refused to talk to me, and this pissed me off. We butted heads and I was astonished at how ungrateful he was being. It made me realize his wounds ran deeper than skin deep. I have learned not to push him, and just wait for the small opportunities to be a part of his life. Dealing with a teenager and his emotions is difficult. Who knows how their brain works? I can see the anger in him, and feel his unhappiness that I live with him. I can only work on myself, my attitude, and my love for him. I can only keep giving, because if I pull away I lose. The other day he had a job interview at Starbucks, I gave him one of my brand new shirts I just bought. It was a nice short sleeved, black polo collared shirt. It still had the tags on it. I walked into his room, but he wouldn't respond to me. I told him, "Good luck on your interview Son. I have a brand new shirt for you." He said nothing so I left it on his chair, I knew he would use it. Later that night when I returned home, I saw him wearing the shirt. I asked him how the interview went; he shrugged me off, but I responded with a smile, sending him love. I was pleased just to know that I helped him look good for his interview. If that was all I was going to receive, at least in a small way I was there with him. Through the midst of all this, one thing I have learned is to just accept life, and try to find the positive that balances out each negative.

August came and my heart sank. I found out that after being busted by the DEA I would lose my license to cosmetology. I felt numb; it just added another layer to my cave. I thought to myself, "I could get upset, I could cry, I could scream and yell, but I just sat here quietly." I sat amazed at what this year had brought to me. Here is an excerpt from my journal: "I am sad, yet I am free. I look to my uncertain future with gratefulness. What a twist of fate that I will now be losing my only job. This is a big blow. I will have to get back into the medical marijuana business. I am grateful to be a yoga instructor. I now know I will survive. I know it will be a hard struggle. I must embrace the uncertainty of my future. I must not think about what has brought me to my knees, I must see through the thick fog, see through the darkness, and somewhere in there I will see the light once again. I will rise once again. I will love and be loved. This has been a snowfall, although most would see it as an avalanche of despair. I have no choice but to face the change. I sit here numb to the world exploring my options. I am facing a three-year sentence, time in prison, and now the loss of my state license. The light within the darkness is my yoga. In yoga all this is like water on my back; it rolls right off of me. Life has a funny way of pushing you into different directions. Filing bankruptcy and losing all my homes pushed me into the medical marijuana business. This year's events pushed me back into the hair business, only to be pushed back out again. Luckily, I just finished my yoga schooling, and am now a certified instructor. Maybe the universe is pushing me in this direction. I have an estimated year to see if I really will lose my license. It is weird; it's almost as if I have no sorrow left in me. What will be, will be. I must now indulge in my yoga teaching, my new path. Losing my license would be an ugly blow, but I know I will survive. My life is not what I dreamed it to be, but through yoga I find peace. In one's darkest hour, your inner light will shine through to guide you on the path you are meant to be." I was struggling to find an end to this book, I felt I had writers block. I didn't write for a couple months after that. Now I realize why; the book wasn't over yet. I was still learning to appreciate my ex-wife. I had to continue my friendship and respect for her.

Chapter 9: Blood Moon Eclipse

September 28 was a Saturday morning and all over the news was the sensation of the blood moon eclipse. This was a once in 33 year event. That morning the mood seemed to be ok; I made myself breakfast: two sausages, two eggs, and a tortilla. I made my lunch for the day: nuts, fruits, veggies, and a sandwich with hot peppers. Off to work I went. The day seemed to go as planned, and at 1 pm I left work and headed to my 2 pm yoga teacher training extensions program. I was taking this training not only to learn how to teach yoga, but to rebuild my confidence after the year's events. It also gave me a sanctuary; a place to go besides my ex-wife's and work. For the last ten years of my life, yoga had been my one place of constant happiness. It was where I could go feeling stressed out, depressed, lonely or sad, and emerge a beacon of light and strength. Some days my day would be so bad I would go to three yoga classes in a day. It would exhaust me, but it would keep me from drinking (a depressant that keeps me from staying motivated). Learning to teach yoga is challenging and nerve wracking. I have been a hair stylist for over twenty years, and I am used to talking to people one on one. But being in front of a multitude of people adds stress and expectations. Your mind starts to play tricks on you. You actually start to judge yourself. What if they don't like me? What if I mess up? What if I freeze or forget? You are live, and guiding ten to thirty people who are looking at you for direction and energy. It was challenging, fun, nerve wracking, and adventurous. I met a great group of people, and realized yoga was a part of my journey for the rest of my life. Yoga has taught me the ability to let things go. To not take things so personally. After finishing my yoga training that day, I decided to stay for a hot power fusion class. The class is heated to 105 degrees. You are doing yoga in a hot sweaty room for an hour. The heat gives your muscles relaxation and flexibility. It increases blood flow, and helps you breathe deeper. I felt great after class, and then headed home, looking forward to the two Sculpin beers I had in the refrigerator. Upon arriving home around 6:30pm at night, I started to cook dinner for the kids. I had a few New York steaks, baked potatoes, chili beans, seared veggies, and a fresh salad. After dinner I saw we were low on food, and I went to the store. My ex-wife asked that I get her a few bottles of wine. I had moved back into her house in the middle of June, and it was now the end of September. The last three and a half months, we were actually getting along. Everyone I knew was amazed. I myself couldn't believe it. I had finally learned to not engage when my ex-wife became crazy. At times it was hard to keep my mouth shut, but I knew I was a guest in her house. My oldest son would usually just give me dirty looks. Often we would argue and he would ask me to move out and find my own place. He was being very inconsiderate and uncaring. But when he needed new tires, his for runner fixed, new clothes, or even money to take his girlfriend out, he would ask me. He was 18, acting like a man, but couldn't pay his own way. He would say mean things like "This is my house, not your house." I would tell him "Son, it is because of me your mother has this house. I have paid for this house and you for the last 18 years." He would then get really disrespectful and call me a loser. Even though he loathed me, I still understood that he was too immature to realize what I was going through. I realized I was the adult, and I had to rise above him to teach him. As teenagers we can't possibly understand that our parents are human; they make mistakes, and most of them try their hardest to be the best parents possible. It is a learning process. He would get in my face, puff up his chest, and confront me. I would let it go and simply say, "Son if you don't like me, then don't ask for my help." This would infuriate him, because it made him realize he still needed me. Even though he would act this way, I would still jump at the chance to help him in hopes that one day by helping him, he might change his mind and open his heart about me. I hoped he would see the truth; to see the good in me. This was the most difficult and volatile part about living at my ex-wife's house. I was a guest in the house I once owned and still paid for; a stranger in my own home. I was a stranger to my oldest son. Each day I would try to understand, forgive, and pick away at the huge iceberg between us. The iceberg built strategically by his mother.

Chapter 10: The Black Widow

Alia is my ex-wife's lesbian lover/girlfriend. During our divorce my ex-wife and Alia met and quickly became friends. Alia had a severe drinking problem, and had lost everything in her life; her job, friends, etc (similar to what I was going through). Shortly after meeting, Alia moved into the house with my ex-wife and my two sons. At first this bothered me, but I knew I had no say in her house. I would go to my sons' basketball games and see them together, and get embarrassed for my sons. My ex-wife would always say they were just friends, but for six years they slept in the same bed together. I knew better than this. Alia looked and acted like a man; with a cropped short black haircut and always wearing pants. She had a slightly overprotective, jealous streak about her. It didn't really bother me because at the time I refused to even speak with my ex-wife. I just had pity on my children for how confused their mother was. I knew in my heart I did not love this woman. Every time I would let my guard down, she would always find a way to "F" me over. Even in this story! Alia and my boys became friends. One day my sons found her having a grand mal seizure on the kitchen floor, and their mom called 911. This was Alia life turning point; it made her realize how much she indulged in alcohol. Flat broke, Alia eventually moved out, but maintained a relationship with my ex-wife and my sons. I could see Alia did a lot for the boys. She cared for their wellbeing, often buying them groceries or burritos with her own money. Alia knew how self-indulgent my ex-wife was, how she would often rather buy herself something than put food in the fridge for my sons. My ex-wife would spoil her dogs Goldie and Blanca and let my sons fend for themselves. She never made breakfast, lunch, or dinner for them. Everything was frozen or microwavable. She was mommy dearest. But she still managed to make them hate me.

Saturday before the blood moon eclipse My ex-wife was acting very irrationally. I could sense something had changed. Alia had been coming over more frequently and waiting on her hand and foot. My ex-wife told the boys she was not gay, but I knew she was confused. Alia was basically my ex-wife's servant. She brought her Starbucks and flowers, took the dogs to the groomers, and basically did anything my ex-wife needed. That Saturday night, my ex-wife started drinking wine. As she polished off the first bottle and started on the second, something changed in her. It was right before the blood moon eclipse, and we were both lying in her bed, watching TV. She started to nag and blame me for my oldest son hating me. My ex-wife took no responsibility for her part and how she manipulated the kids. She kept telling me I had anger issues and emotional problems. I asked her to stop. She continued for thirty minutes. I finally yelled at her, "Shut the "F" up." Lying there, I realized I truly hated this woman. Even though I have learned to forgive and appreciate her, she still treated me as her servant. I cleaned the house, did the laundry, took out the trash, kept the dishes done, cleaned the kitchen, and paid rent. I was the one who made our children dinner while she laid in bed on her fat ass of laziness. She would bark orders from her bed, and I would get irritated. I started to realize that I had grown, I had learned to appreciate. I had matured. But she remained the same: a delusional, lazy, greedy, selfish woman.

Sunday the blood moon eclipse was beautiful. The colors of red and orange and the exactness of the eclipse was phenomenal, a true gift of nature. Monday after the eclipse my ex-wife was sick and irritated. She started barking orders. I sat on the couch after cooking Christopher's breakfast and making him lunch and taking him to school. I realized she was sick so I didn't respond to her barks. She left for work and I was thankful. When she returned home from work that day, I could tell she didn't feel well so I made her tea and made dinner for the boys. Tuesday was the big blow out. The day started like many others. I woke up and made Christopher lunch and took him to school. My ex-wife woke up and started barking orders. I sat on the couch and in a nice voice said to my ex-wife, "I am not Alia. I am not your servant. I pay rent to stay here. If you want things done, then you need to get out of your bed and help get them done." She did not like this. She ignored me and left for work irritated. I realized Dante had his friend over; they were in his room playing videos and smoking his vape. I walked in and found them taking shots of tequila at 10:30 am. I gathered my boxes of paperwork to bring to the tax guy. I returned home at 1:30 pm to find my ex-wife and Alia at the house. My ex-wife was in a bad mood, and even Alia couldn't stand her. Alia and I both walked out of the house, each looking at each other, and she stated how selfish my ex-wife could be. I laughed and put a finger to my head in a fun gun gesture, and pulled the trigger. We both laughed, and I said, "You can have her; she is miserable to be around." I came back in and put my box of tax paperwork in Christopher's newly cleaned out room, and stacked the tax boxes neatly in the closet. My ex-wife pushed open the door and started yelling at me, "I don't want anything in this room." I explained I needed to have access to my papers and Dante was giving me attitude for having my stuff in his room. I told her my things would only be here for a day or two and my court date was the next day, when I would learn whether or not I was going to prison. I knew the D.A. was on my case, and I was facing three years with three consecutive sentences for selling marijuana to an undercover agent (even though I had my medical marijuana card, and my medical collective paperwork). I asked her to leave me alone and she started yelling at me in her frantic irritating voice. I told her she was being a rude "b" and she exploded. She started yelling, "You called me a "b"?"

And proceeded to run through the house screaming, "Your father is calling me a "b", in my own house!" All I was trying to do was install a clothing rack in Christopher's closet and set my box of tax papers there. My ex-wife kept on yelling until Dante came into the room. He puffed up his chest, stood in my face, and said, "Why don't you just leave and go get your own place? You don't belong here." I asked him to leave the room. I know that it is only natural for him to want to protect his mother. My ex-wife was still being dramatic so I went to Dante's room to look for a saw to cut the clothing rack bar. Dante followed me into his room and got in my face, telling me to get out and that I had no right to call his mom names. I turned around and stuck my finger in his face and said, "I am sick and tired of you disrespecting me." He pushed my hand from his face, and I could tell this was escalating so I wrapped him up and took him to the ground. He was trying to hit me, screaming "Get the "F" off of me." His mother heard us arguing and came running in. She jumped on my back and started scratching my face, my ribs, and my arms. I tried to explain to her that I was just holding him and I wasn't hitting him; I was just waiting until he calmed down. She proceeded to dial 911. I couldn't believe this woman. This whole day was manipulated and orchestrated by her. She started an argument about a box of taxes in a closet, and now this. She told 911 I attacked my son. I was amazed at how she could manipulate any situation to turn it around on me. This day, the blood moon eclipse, the day before my court fate, the last thing I needed was to face an abuse charge. I would have gone to prison no questions asked.

That day my hatred came back for this woman. I gathered my immediate things and started to walk out. I told them I didn't want to be in this place of dark energy where my family keeps taking from me without any appreciation. As I opened the door to leave I told her to please have my $12,200 ready in her safe for me to retrieve later. She said it was in the bank. I asked her "Please go get it, I will need it to pay bills and get an apartment. I also need to pay the state board to keep my license for cosmetology." With a smirk in her eye she said "OK." This was bad. Now I understood why she was acting this way. I then realized that this woman never really changed. Finding forgiveness for her was one-sided. She was an evil mommy dearest, a black widow. I knew something had happened with the money, and that's when my appreciation for this woman died. The black widow had shown her true colors. Her red underbelly was clearly showing. She had laid out her web of manipulation and distracted me with fake caring. She opened her door to me, but secretly lured me in, to eat me. She spent all of my $12,200 that was in her safe to pay her mortgage, and collected a monthly rent of $922 from me. I also paid for SDG&E bills, $500 a month on food for the boys, and $500 a month for their fun for each month I stayed there. I bought them clothes, and a 1,000 graduation gift. I spent over $1,000 repairing her house. I spent $9,000 from June until the end of September. I got eaten alive and spit out by this black widow of a woman. This whole web of illusion was just an act. An act for her selfish gain. She stole my hard-earned money. She took every last cent I had to my name. Then she orchestrated the argument in which my oldest son confronted me, calling 911, almost ensuring I would go to prison. She reverted back to her crazy ass selfish attitude. Oh, but I was the one with the anger issues and the violent streak. Everything was my fault because I was the angry person. She was always planting mental bombs. This is the poison and pus coming from the black widow. I am the scorpion, backed into the corner, with the black widow spinning her web surrounding me. My stinger is arched up high waiting for the precise moment to defend myself. The black widow keeps frantically and dramatically spinning her web of illusions, to ensnare me and suck my blood dry (money). She took everything for herself and said it was for the children. This book is a scorpion stinger, and it has struck back at the precise moment and time.

About the Author

DAVID PEREZ, world renowned MASTER HAIR DESIGNER, AUTHOR and ENTREPRENEUR started his writing as a personal memoir, which in turn became this most exciting and riveting book about appreciation, forgiveness and moving forward. David has been a celebrity hair stylist for over 20 years, working on actors including Benicio Del Toro, Dennis Franz, as well as super models for on-location photo shoots. Using his creative genius David is starting a new adventure in his life. Originally from Los Angeles, California, he now lives in San Diego and Los Angeles. One of David's specialties is hair extensions; he is in the process of writing a book on sex appeal with hair extensions, and how to color your hair and look like a celebrity. With over 25 years as a master hair designer and color specialist, David loves to make women beautiful. Now he is a man on a mission, setting an example to his two wonderful and loving sons, showing them greatness comes from within, and the true measure of a man is how he gets back up after life events brought him to his knees.

44666867R00069

Made in the USA
San Bernardino, CA
20 July 2019